Ministry and Education
in Conversation

Ministry and Education in Conversation

Edited by
Mary C. Boys

Saint Mary's Press
Christian Brothers Publications
Winona, Minnesota

Cover design by Roderick Robertson, FSC

ISBN: 0-88489-126-7
Library of Congress Catalog Card Number: 80-53204

Copyright 1981 by Saint Mary's Press,
Terrace Heights, Winona, Minnesota 55987

Contents

Introduction

by Mary C. Boys, SNJM

A musician friend of mine once emerged after a practice session to ask whether she should be encouraged or discouraged that she had made new mistakes rather than merely repeated the old ones. Today's Church has a similar situation; in managing to overcome some of the blunders of the past, we inevitably risk creating new dilemmas.

A case in point is religious education. For years it was generally regarded as theology's ugly stepsister or as education's foster child. Unable to lay claim to their own identity, religious educators floundered from fad to fad without engaging in any comprehensive inquiry into foundational issues. Only in recent years have they begun to devote themselves to developing a corpus of literature as the basis of an emerging discipline.[1]

But just as religious education began to grow into its own person, so to speak, it was met by a new child: **ministry.**[2] Ministry enjoyed the limelight of the newcomer; individuals who had once been hired as religious educators now pronounced that they were "into ministry." Moreover, the term became as inflated as the economy: there was the ministry of ushering, the ministry of music, the ministry of collection-counting, the ministry of coffee and doughnuts. Not only did the stage seem set for a classic case of sibling rivalry, but the term appeared perilously close to losing any meaning because of such vacuous usage.

Clearly the need existed for some penetrating examination of the meaning of this recent arrival (at least in Roman Catholic circles) and its relationship with religious education. The papers in this volume are intended precisely to provide such a serious scrutiny.

The Genesis of the Papers

The publication of this analysis of the relationship between ministry and education results from a symposium at Boston College. Religious education has long been the subject of inquiry and interest at Boston College; in 1971 it inaugurated an "Institute for the Study of Religious Education and Service" as a six-week summer graduate program. Over the years it came to offer an academic year program as well, offering three degrees (M.Ed., C.A.E.S., and Ph.D.) in religious education. But repeated requests for courses and programs in ministry led the Institute to launch an M.A. program in pastoral ministry in 1978 and to change its name to the "Institute of Religious Education and Pastoral Ministry."

The Institute is committed to supporting and contributing to the development of foundational literature in religious education. An outcome of this pledge has been the sponsorship of symposia to generate, analyze, and evaluate fundamental questions. The first symposium, in April 1977, was devoted to identifying and clarifying basic issues in religious education from a Roman Catholic perspective; the second, in April 1978, sought the wisdom of Protestant colleagues as well in examining the relationship between handing on a religious tradition and changing the world.[3]

The papers in this volume represent the edited version of the third symposium, "The Intersection of Ministry and Education," in November 1979. The topic emerged as a direct by-product of the Institute's new program in pastoral ministry, having surfaced repeatedly during attempts to compose a statement of purposes and objectives. The animated discussion during this formulation of policy, as well as the subsequent lack of perspicuity, suggested the value of inviting other scholars to address the issue.

The Symposium

Invitations were extended to four prominent scholars representing not only different fields of study but varying geographical settings as well: Sandra M. Schneiders, Assistant Professor of New Testament and Spirituality at the Jesuit School of Theology of the Graduate Theological Union in Berkeley; Virgil P. Elizondo, a pastoral theologian and President of the Mexican American Cultural Center in San Antonio; Sara Butler, a systematic theologian, ecumenical specialist, and a General Councillor for the Missionary Sisters of the Blessed Trinity in Philadelphia; and Robert Wood Lynn, Vice-President for Religion of the Lilly Endowment and former Professor of Religion and Education at Union Theological Seminary in New York City. Lynn, who described himself as a "six-foot, six-inch Protestant postscript to the panel," contributed not only his expertise as a historian of religious education, but also his keen insight into Catholic dilemmas. The final member of the panel, Richard P. McBrien, then Professor of Theology at Boston College and the Director of its Institute of Religious Education and Pastoral Ministry, served as moderator and critic. His paper, written after the symposium itself, develops ideas he proffered during various discussions.

The entire focus, however, was not reserved for the panelists, lest their discussion remain uninformed by the comments and questions of the participants. In fact, considerable attention was given to developing a suitable format for the symposium so as to ensure a high quality of discussion. Such efforts had likewise characterized the previous two symposia, but were intensified in the light of Dwayne Huebner's concluding paper of the symposium in 1978. Huebner, concerned about the social division of labor in which academicians made presentations and practitioners simply listened and raised questions, asked: "What do we know about how the practitioners of religious education speak about their work and their experiences, or how the students speak about their experiences?"[4]

Taking Huebner's admonition seriously, the Institute faculty structured a process in which the participants (approximately ninety people, including Institute students from Australia, New Zealand, Nigeria, and Indonesia), who had received the papers for study beforehand, had the opportunity not merely to raise questions from the floor following a panelist's presentation, but to press for implications, criticize, and raise fresh points of view. As a result, the exchange among panelists and participants was crisp. Something of the flavor of the discussion may be garnered from McBrien's paper, which makes frequent reference to issues raised during the day-and-a-half session. The importance of the dialogical structure is eloquently attested to in Sandra Schneiders' paper; following the symposium, she returned home to write a substantial

"Afterword" as a means of contributing a systematic reflection on the issues which had arisen during discussion.

Readers may wish to construct their own dialogical process by utilizing the "Questions for Discussion" which I have formulated and placed at the conclusion of each panelist's paper. (No discussion questions have been appended to Richard McBrien's paper because it already contains many questions.) Indeed, those who study this volume with care may find it of immense value in identifying key issues, raising tough-minded questions, and demonstrating methodological procedures whereby complex matters might be investigated.

The Issues

In his summary and critique, Richard McBrien identifies four major clusters of questions which consistently appear in both the papers and the ensuing discussions: (1) the identity of the religious educator vis-à-vis the minister; (2) the call of the community to ministry; (3) the role of culture in shaping the understanding and practice of ministry; and (4) the criteria of a true Christian spirituality for ministry. His recognition of these basic issues may serve as a conceptual framework within which to compare and contrast each paper.

Apropos of the title of this volume, it may be helpful to delineate each panelist's formulation of the relationship of ministry to education. Schneiders stipulates Christian education to mean all forms of witness to the Gospel, classifying it as one of the Church's ministries, and equating it with the "ministry of the Word." While leaving ministry as such undefined, she describes the ministry of the Word in terms of its function of evoking, sustaining, nurturing, and challenging faith. Elizondo uses both education and ministry in their dictionary definitions: the former being viewed as the provision for schooling or a formal course of study, and the latter as a service or function, often associated with religion, which is performed for another. Sara Butler uses ministry in its broad sense as almost any service rendered in the Lord's name for the Kingdom; this implies for her a posture of service inseparable from attentiveness to another in faith. She utilizes, however, the distinction between **ministries** as charisms of the communities and the **Minis-**

try of the ordained. Education in Butler's view embraces almost any process that leads to human growth and development towards maturity, regardless of the setting in which it takes place. Ministry is for her the more general term under which education ought to fall.

Robert Lynn takes a different approach. Rather than defining each term and formulating its relation to the other, he instead assumes an historian's perspective and narrates the account of the reduction of both education and ministry to church management. McBrien, who notes each panelist's formulation, himself refrains from articulating one. He has, however, defined ministry in his recent work, **Catholicism,** as a service designated publicly or explicitly by the Church to assist it in the fulfillment of its mission.[5]

In general, it may be observed that the panelists devoted more attention to discussion of ministry than to education. While only one, Virgil Elizondo, seemed content to limit education to schooling, none of the others seemed cognizant either of the classic definitions of education (such as John Dewey's view of it as the "reconstruction of experience" or Lawrence Cremin's specification of education as the "deliberate, systematic, and sustained effort to transmit, evoke, or acquire knowledge, attitudes, skills, or sensibilities, as well as any outcome of that effort")[6] or of the precise historical referents of the multiplicity of terms in religious education—e.g., catechetics, Catholic education, religious instruction, religious education, Christian education.[7] Perhaps because each of the panelists, with the exception of Robert Lynn, works more in the realm of theology and ministry than in education and ministry, none addressed what it might mean for the Church to make a long-term commitment to education. That education in its own right was not dealt with in any substantial fashion may in some measure account for the fact that both Schneiders and Butler subsume it under ministry and that Elizondo largely ignores it. Had there been more time, it might have proved illuminating to pose Gabriel Moran's contention that we need to be bilingual, that is, that we need to speak both an ecclesiastical language (theology, ministry) and an educational language.[8] Both languages are necessary; neither excludes nor exhausts the other. Had education been given more attention in the papers, it is possible that the relationship of education to ministry might have been viewed as a complementary one.[9]

But the purpose of the symposium was to raise issues, to prune away imprecise language, to exemplify methodologies, and to engage both academicians and practitioners in serious, sustained conversation. If neither perfect clarity nor total consensus was reached, then it may at least be consoling to note poet John Ciardi's admission that "I prefer my confusions to the Pentagon's clarity."[10] Indeed, the very complexity of the issues as analyzed herein may be of value precisely insofar as the difficulties endow us with genuine modesty about our own perspectives and with a reluctance to forge ahead hastily.

A former professor once accused his fellow theologians of too often rationalizing their jargon by "baptizing muddles into mysteries." Whatever the limitations of Boston College's third symposium on "The Intersection of Ministry and Education," it successfully avoided such a temptation.

NOTES

1. See D. Huebner, "Education in the Church," **Andover Newton Quarterly** 12 (1972):122-129; B. Marthaler, "A Discipline in Quest of an Identity: Religious Education," **Horizons** 3 (1976):203-215; R. P. McBrien, "Toward an American Catechesis," **The Living Light** 13 (1976):167-181; C. J. Melchert, "What Is Religious Education?" **The Living Light** 14 (1977):339-353; J. Westerhoff, ed., **Who Are We? The Quest for a Religious Education** (Birmingham: Religious Education Press, 1978); J. M. Lee, **The Shape of Religious Instruction** (Dayton: Pflaum, 1971) and **The Flow of Religious Instruction** (Dayton: Pflaum, 1973); and M. J. Taylor, ed., **Foundations for Christian Education in an Era of Change** (Nashville: Abingdon, 1976), pp. 30-40.

2. After the Religious Education Association was formed in 1903, it began its own journal, **Religious Education.** Now ministry, too, has its magazine, the monthly **Ministry,** published by Winston Press in Minneapolis.

3. Symposium panelists Thomas H. Groome, James Michael Lee, Berard Marthaler, Gabriel Moran, and Francoise Darcy-Berube contributed the essays in 1977; their work is available in P. O'Hare, ed., **Foundations of Religious Education** (New York: Paulist, 1978). The essays in 1978 were authored by Mary Boys, Maria Harris, C. Ellis Nelson, Letty Russell, and Dwayne Huebner; they are collected in P. O'Hare, ed., **Tradition and Transformation in Religious Education** (Birmingham: Religious Education Press, 1979).

4. D. Huebner, "The Language of Religious Education," in **Tradition and Transformation,** p. 93.

5. R. P. McBrien, **Catholicism** (Minneapolis: Winston Press, 1980), p. 845.

6. See J. Dewey, **Experience and Education** (New York: Collier, 1938), p. 89; L. Cremin, **Traditions of American Education** (New York: Basic Books, 1977), p. 158.

7. A brief word on terminology. "Catechetics" is a term generally Catholic in usage in which education is subsumed under the pastoral mission of the Church; it refers to that aspect of the ministry of the Word "which leads both communities and individual members of the faithful to maturity of faith." **General Catechetical Directory** (Washington, D.C.: USCC, 1971) #21; cf. **Sharing the Light of Faith: A National Catechetical Directory for Catholics of the United States** (Washington, D.C.: USCC, 1979). "Church education" implies schooling in religious matters under the aegis of church sponsorship; "religious instruction" originated as J. M. Lee's term for the "conscious and deliberative facilitation of specified behavioral goals" ("Foreword," in Lee and P. C. Rooney, eds., **Toward a Future for Religious Education** [Dayton: Pflaum, 1970], p. 1). "Religious education" appears to have the broadest and most ecumenical usage, as it denotes an educational concern for the religious aspects of a person's or a community's life. "Christian education," on the other hand, more narrowly refers to that concern for handing on the faith that grew out of Protestant neo-orthodoxy.

8. G. Moran, "The Two Languages of Religious Education," **The Living Light** 14 (1977):7-15.

9. A view I have developed briefly in "Ministry and Education: Scriptural Perspectives," **The Living Light** 16 (1979):313-326.

10. J. Ciardi, "Manner of Speaking," **Saturday Review** 5 (1977):56.

The Ministry of the Word and Contemporary Catholic Education

by Sandra M. Schneiders, IHM

AUTOBIOGRAPHICAL STATEMENT

My interest in religion, which goes back as far as I can remember, took shape as an interest in theology during my first year in college. The following year, 1955, I joined the religious congregation of the Sisters, Servants of the Immaculate Heart of Mary, and immediately came under the influence of an inspiring teacher, Margaret Brennan, IHM, who awakened in me the twin interests which have been the focus of my work since then: Sacred Scripture and Christian Spirituality.

Personnel needs of the congregation led to my finishing the B.A. with a major in sociology. My senior research project on the work of Talcott Parsons was an invaluable introduction to high-level theoretical reflection, but I had no real love for the field of sociology and was happy to find my way back into my field of predilection as a religion teacher in grade and high school. Congregational needs led to my earning the M.A. in philosophy at the University of Detroit in 1967 with a specialization in metaphysics. Philosophy was much closer to my real interests than sociology had been, and I probably learned more philosophy in the two years that I taught it at Marygrove College in Detroit than I did in the library preparing my thesis on the metaphysics of freedom in Jacques Maritain.

In 1968 I had the opportunity to pursue my deepest interest. The next three years were spent in Paris where I received the S.T.L. in 1971 from the Institut Catholique with a specialization in patristics. Those years provided the immensely enriching experience of learning to think in a foreign language, an experience which germinated in succeeding years into a deep interest in the problem of interpretation of language.

After a year of teaching theology in the United States (1971-72), I returned to Europe, this time to Rome where I spent three and a half years studying for the S.T.D. in New Testament, which was granted by the Gregorian University in 1975. My studies included course work at the Biblical Institute and were done within the framework of the relatively new program in Christian Spirituality of the Gregorian. I had the privilege of studying with teachers whose interests, perspectives, and scholarship shaped my own work decisively: Raymond Brown, Rudolf Schnackenburg, Gilles Cusson, among others. I was most influenced, however, by my dissertation director, Edward Malatesta, whose own work combined a scientifically rigorous New Testament scholarship with an equally solid and scholarly approach to Christian Spirituality. After defending my dissertation, **The Resurrection Narrative in John 20,** I returned to the United States and began teaching New Testament and Spirituality at the Jesuit School of Theology in the Graduate Theological Union in Berkeley, California, where I was also the chief administrator of a one-year program in Spirituality and facilitator of the new doctoral program in Christian Spirituality of the GTU.

My continuing interest in how the Scriptures function in the religious life of believing individuals and the Christian community gradually came into sharper focus as an interest in hermeneutics, and a grant from the Association of Theological Schools (1978) enabled me to spend six months on research leave at the University of St. Michael's College in Toronto acquiring a basic knowledge of contemporary hermeneutical theory in preparation for work in the area of biblical hermeneutics. Since returning to Berkeley in the fall of 1979, I have continued to pursue this interest in my teaching, research, and writing and see it opening out on ever wider vistas. Hermeneutics appears to be the area in which all my interests meet, and it will surely be the arena of my work for several years to come.

Sandra M. Schneiders, IHM

"Christian education" is not a New Testament term but it is a New Testament reality, the activity designated as the "ministry of the Word."[1] If the purpose of this symposium is, in part, to clarify the

relationship between ministry and education, we can begin by saying that education is one of the ministries through which the Church has, from the very beginning, lived the mission which it has and is,[2] namely, effectively proclaiming God's reconcilation of the world to God in Jesus Christ.[3]

Not only is the ministry of the Word **one** of the Church's ministries but the New Testament leaves little room for doubt that it is the Church's primary ministry. Jesus frequently expressed his own understanding of his mission in terms of "bearing witness to the truth" (John 18:37), "preaching" (Mark 1:38), and "evangelizing the poor" (Matt. 11:5). He was perceived by both his friends and his enemies primarily as a teacher and, though he performed remarkable deeds of healing, it was not primarily for his works but for his teaching that he was finally condemned to death (cf. Matt. 26:59-68; Mark 14:61-64; Luke 23:2-5; John 18:19-24). Both during his lifetime and after the Resurrection, Jesus commissioned his disciples to preach the Gospel by word and confirming act (cf. Matt. 10:5-33; Luke 10:1-12; Matt. 28:18-20; Mark 16:15-18;[4] Luke 24:46-48; Acts 1:8).[5]

It is clear from the Acts of the Apostles, as well as from the writings of Paul and the earliest non-canonical writings that have been preserved, that the first generation Church understood its mission primarily in terms of preaching the Gospel. Peter's first act, when the power of the Spirit was given to the infant Church, was to address the word of the Gospel to the crowds who had come to Jerusalem for the Jewish Feast of Pentecost (Acts 2:14-42). Neither threats (Acts 4:18-21,29) nor punishment (Acts 4:17-21; 40-42) deterred the first disciples from witnessing in the Holy City to what God had done in Jesus and, when persecution dispersed the Jerusalem community, "those who were scattered went about preaching the Word" (Acts 8:4) in Samaria, Galilee, and Judea.

The sense of the primacy of the ministry of the Word within this earliest community as well as without appears in the account of the conflict between the "Hellenists" and the "Hebrews" in Acts 6:1-6. The Hellenist Christians in the Jerusalem community voiced a complaint to the Twelve about the inadequate attention to the material needs of their widows. The Twelve replied, "It is not right that we should give up preaching the Word of God to serve tables. Therefore . . . pick out from among you seven men of good repute, full of the Spirit and of wisdom, whom we may appoint to this duty. But we will devote ourselves to prayer and to the ministry of the Word'' (Acts 6:1-2).[6]

Paul understood his own election and mission as a binding vocation to preach the Gospel (Rom. 1:1, 14:18-20; 1 Cor. 4:15, 9:15-17), and in the one passage in which he ranks the charisms given to the Church by the Spirit he says, "God has appointed in the Church first apostles, second prophets, third teachers" (1 Cor. 12:28). All other ministerial gifts, such as the working of miracles, healing, administration, and glossolalia, are secondary to the three forms of ministry of the Word: evangelization, prophecy, and teaching.

We find this same primacy attached to the ministry of the Word in the Church's earliest "catechism," the **Didache** or **The Teaching of the Twelve Apostles.**[7] This document, dating from the early second century, repeatedly singles out prophets and teachers as the most essential ministers in the community, even basing the reverence owed by the community to bishops and deacons on the participation of these latter in the ministry of the prophets and teachers.[8] It specifies that the prophets and teachers are to be supported by the community and even regarded as the community's "high priests."[9]

These few selections from the Gospels, the Acts of the Apostles, the writings of Paul, and the **Didache** suffice to indicate the primacy of the ministry of the Word in the mission-consciousness of the early Church. In our own times when the social apostolate seems to have a clear ministerial priority over Catholic education, we cannot help wondering if the priority assigned by the early Church to the ministry of the Word was not simply a function of a different historical situation, or even the expression of a certain implicit gnostic dualism that equated salvation with knowledge. In the following paragraphs I would like to discuss the meaning of the ministry of the Word in hopes of contributing to a more adequate understanding of the **nature** and **function** of Christian education as ministry and of the implications of such a contemporary understanding for a renewed praxis.

The priority of the ministry of the Word arises directly from its relation to faith and the centrality of faith to Christian experience. Salvation, however it is understood in detail, consists somehow in the union of humanity with God, the participation of people individually and communally in divine life. The initiative of this sharing of divine life rests with God, who, according to Christian belief, has freely chosen to communicate Godself to us in a multitude of ways, culminating in the life, ministry, and paschal mystery of Jesus the Christ. God's self-communication, in other words, is not primarily mystical, that is, a direct and unmediated union, but rather a communication mediated by events of history, most notably by the event of Jesus. Herein lies the importance of the Word, for it is the Word which witnesses to God's self-revelation in history. The word of witness points out the presence and action of God in persons and events, calls for recognition of that action, and challenges the one who sees to respond to God's self-gift with the gift of him or herself. According to Mark, Jesus' ministry opens with just such a word of witness: "The time is now, the saving action of God is present here, repent and believe in the Good News" (Mark 1:15).[10]

The first Christians, of course, transferred Jesus' proclamation of the "kingdom" or "reign," that is, of the "saving action" of God, to Jesus himself in whose resurrection they saw the full expression of that saving action. They witnessed to Jesus first as the object of God's saving action (Acts 2:32) and finally as the subject of that salvific action for all who believe (Acts 2:36). This is the primary meaning of the proclamation that God has made Jesus Lord and Christ.[11]

Now faith is the response to the word of witness; it is the acceptance of God's salvation in Jesus and thus the entrance into the divine life of love.[12] Faith is the root, if you will, of Christian identity which is constituted and expressed by love lived in hope. Because God's self-communication has the modality it has, that is, because it takes place in human experience, it must be witnessed to in order to be perceived. Faith depends on this witness and thus the entire adventure of Christian life, not only in its inception but in its growth and expression, is dependent on the ministry of the Word. Obviously, witness is given in many ways. Actions sometimes witness more clearly than words. It is also obvious that the word of witness functions differently at various moments in a person's faith life. Apostolic proclamation evokes faith and calls to initial and ongoing conversion; prophecy brings the Word to bear upon experience to interpret it and call us to responsible action; teaching brings experience to bear upon the Word to enlighten it and set it free to reveal, in each age and place, the full scope of God's promise and the Gospel's challenge. And as the Word finds a home in the one to whom witness is given, this disciple in turn becomes a witness by word and life to others. Thus, in a very real sense, the ministry of the Word is the task of all the members of the Church,[13] even though certain exercises of that ministry, notably teaching in the formal sense, tend to be exercised primarily by those prepared for this specialized task.

In summary, then, the primacy of the ministry of the Word has nothing to do with intellectualism or gnostic notions of salvation. It arises from the fact that faith, the free response to God's saving self-gift to us in Jesus, must be evoked, nurtured, sustained, and challenged by the witness of disciples who have come to believe and are therefore able to point out to others God's presence and action in human experience. The primacy of the ministry of the Word is a function of the centrality of faith in Christian experience.

Why, then, does that ministry seem so ineffectual today that many have abandoned it in favor of other ministries which seem more evangelical, more effective, in the simplest terms, more needed and wanted by people? I would like to propose one reason that might at least open the way for some discussion. Faith has been understood differently at different periods in history or, at least, different aspects of the faith response have had a certain experiential ascendancy in the Church's life at different times.[14] The understanding of the ministry of the Word at any given time is a function of the understanding of faith. I wonder if we are not experiencing at the present time a gap between our real understanding of faith and the understanding of the ministry of the Word which is operative in a good deal of the institutional ministry of the Word, that is, in education, preaching, and seminary formation, with the result that the more deeply committed a given minister is to witnessing to Christ the less he or she is attracted to the institutionalized forms of ministry of the Word.

By way of illustration of this hypothesis let me return once more to the first century. In the earliest days of the Church, faith was understood primarily in terms of the conversion of adults and their coming to share in the life of the Christian community in visible opposition to the surrounding culture. Consequently, the ministry of the Word was understood primarily in terms of

apostleship or evangelization.[15] Paul was the paradigmatic minister of the Word, crisscrossing the known world witnessing to God's
saving action in Jesus and organizing the new converts into communities of faith. The ministers of the Word whom he set up in
these communities or whom the communities appointed were less
teachers in any original or originating sense than residential repre-
sentatives of Paul who were to guard the Word he had preached
(1 Tim. 1:3-4; 2 Tim. 1:13; 2 Tim. 2:2; Titus 1:5). Less than two
centuries later, however, when the Church was already a wide-
spread phenomenon but still the object of severe though intermit-
tent persecution, it was much more concerned with demonstrating
the validity of Christian faith both to its own members, whose
conviction had to withstand the ultimate test of martyrdom, and to
their religio-philosophically inclined non-Christian opponents.
During the second and third centuries we find the paradigmatic
ministry of the Word to be the doing and teaching of theology, both
apologetic and speculative. Faith as conviction unto death and as
adequate interpretation of the world and of human affairs was best
served by the witness of sound and imaginative teaching, and so
Justin Martyr (mid-second century), Clement (c. 150-216), Origen
(c. 185-254), Tertullian (c. 160-220), and Cyprian (c. 200-258)
dominate the scene.

If we jump now to the Counter-Reformation period, in which
the Roman Church was predominantly concerned with preserving
the belief and discipline of its members against the massive threat
of Reformation theology and practice, we find a different aspect of
faith in the ascendancy. Faith was conceived of primarily as intellectual assent to the truth of revelation propositionally formulated.[16] Imaginative speculation and behavioral originality could
not be tolerated by a Church under siege, and fidelity was often
enough equated with rote repetition of doctrinal formulas and strict
conformity to Catholic practice. The primary ministry of the Word,
the ministry which was suited to this understanding of faith, was
the transmission and protection of the faith, that is, the inculcating
of doctrinal conclusions with as much supporting argumentation
as the learner could handle and training in correct practice with as
much motivation to conformity as possible. It is within the context
of this Counter-Reformation understanding of faith that the modern
conception of "Catholic education" developed. Catholic education,

the primary expression of the ministry of the Word, was almost exclusively concerned with the "indoctrination" of Catholic children within a school setting and a parallel (though less thoroughgoing) reinforcement of this education from the pulpit throughout adult life. The commitment of Catholic teachers was high because they saw their apostolate as directly related to the fostering of faith as it was understood by them, by the officials of the Church, by their students, and by Catholic parents. Particularly in the United States, where the Counter-Reformation ecclesiastical mentality was reinforced by minority-immigrant cultural status, the centrality of Catholic education as the primary service of the faith, the paradigmatic ministry of the Word, was evident.

Now, the hypothesis I would like to explore is the following: the contemporary understanding of faith is undergoing a profound shift from the Counter-Reformation model. The shift actually began between the World Wars, reached a surprisingly high level of articulation in Vatican II, and has continued to deepen and become more radical since the Council.[17] Meanwhile, the institutional forms of the ministry of the Word, that is, education in Catholic institutions and Church preaching, have changed far less substantially for reasons we will address below. The result is that the official ministers of the Word, notably Catholic educators, and the ordained in parish situations, often sense a drastic decrease in the real relation between the ministry they exercise and the evoking and fostering of faith as they, along with the rest of the active Church, progressively understand it. The vitality of the ministry of the Word depends upon the perceived reality of the relation between the witness given and the faith response evoked and nurtured. When the witness does not evoke that response, a sense of aimlessness and irrelevance undermines ministerial commitment; and those who are most ministerially alive seek other spheres of service as they try to discover where the real needs are and how those needs can best be met. The degree of ministerial malaise is well expressed by the very existence of a symposium which discusses not the ministry **of** education but "Ministry **and** Education," which reexamines the relationship between these two terms whose connection, much less quasi identity, is no longer clear.

Let us return now to the institutional forms of the ministry of the Word characteristic of the period between the Council of Trent (especially in its post-French Revolution to Vatican I phase) and

Vatican Council II. If faith is understood primarily as intellectual assent to propositions, expressed in active religious practice of a privatized, cultural type, the ideal way to foster it is clearly classroom inculcation and explanation of the propositions in the context of a total school environment in which practice (for example, daily prayers, regular reception of the sacraments, heightened participation in feasts and devotions, etc.) is an integral, pervasive element. It is neither possible nor necessary to examine all the factors that helped to undermine the prevailing pre-Conciliar understanding of faith. We need only allude to such factors as the enormous ferment in Protestant theology in the interwar period as well as to the biblical and liturgical movements which began to affect Catholic theology at the very time that Catholic integration into mainstream culture in America was suggesting to the ordinary believer rich alternatives to Catholic beliefs and practices. Meanwhile, parents' concerns for the educational opportunities and upward mobility of their children started to compete with commitment to confessional formation. And studies began to suggest that Catholic education probably did not produce a notably superior brand of human being, American, or even Catholic, at precisely the time when human development and cultural integration were coming to seem at least as important to many American Catholics as religious proficiency.[18]

The understanding of Catholic faith emergent under these and other influences is not nearly so clear as that of the inter-Conciliar period.[19] For a short period just prior to and immediately after Vatican II, the working definition of faith for many Catholic educators was "personal commitment to Jesus." Since educators realized that commitment cannot be taught the way one teaches doctrine, highly imaginative efforts were made to make religious education less intellectual, or at least less intellectualistic, and more experiential. The setting, however, most often continued to be the classroom, with the minister of the Word functioning primarily as a teacher.

The ministry of the Word in this Conciliar period suffered from at least two major weaknesses which seriously undermined it and effectively prevented its real transformation. First, the conception of faith as personal commitment to Christ represented more the enthusiastic application by American educators of European Protestant theological trends than an indigenous American rethinking of the faith. Its inadequacy might have been less evident in a different time and place, but world problems today and the American position in the world are such that the kerygmatic concept of faith never really took hold. Secondly, despite the correct perception of educators that commitment is not an academic discipline, that it cannot be taught or graded, no real alternative to the school model of ministry of the Word was found. It is one thing to know what does not work; but it is something quite different to find or invent something that does.[20]

This brings us to the crucial question: how can we understand faith today and what kind of ministry of the Word is called for in the contemporary post-Conciliar Church? It seems to me that the answer is emerging if we know how to listen. Where is faith, the integral response to God's saving action on our behalf, most alive and effective? It seems to be in small grassroots communities: charismatic groups, small local groups of religious men or women, life-revision groups, feminist support groups, alternative worshipping communities attached to universities, service groups, groups battling various kinds of addiction, social action groups, and prayer groups of all kinds.[21] What faith seems to be for these people is a kind of hermeneutic, that is, a kind of interpretation which they apply to their everyday experience and then use for personal and social transformation. Faith is not a set of propositions, even less a set of answers. Rather, it is an interpretive key, a perspective, a way of looking at their own reality in the light of the Gospel, which makes sense of that reality in terms of the paschal mystery of Jesus and which impels the interpreter toward faith-action in his or her own world.

The ministry of the Word which will truly serve contemporary faith, it seems to me, is a ministry which facilitates this hermeneutic and its resultant action. This ministry can take the form of supplying resources for the reading of the Gospel, leading or participating in the celebration of the Word to which the reflection gives rise, or supplying spiritual accompaniment and guidance for individuals as they come to grips with the challenges of the Gospel in their own lives. But what it calls for and challenges us to, above all, is to learn to relate reflection and praxis in a new way. Those of us who were raised in a theological tradition in which abstract principles had priority over concrete experience must learn to begin our reflection in praxis, allowing concrete experience to raise and/or refine our questions and to point the direction of the answers. In philosophical terms we must enter the hermeneutical circle at the point of experience rather than at the point of theory.[22] In this respect we have a great deal to learn from liberation theologians, black theologians, feminist theologians, psychological and sociological analysts, from all whose life experience has led them to ask new questions of the Scriptures and to be dissatisfied with old answers.[23]

With those observations we return to the question with which we started, namely the **nature, function,** and **interrelation** of education and ministry. Education is a dimension of the ministry of the Word which, from the beginning, has been the Church's most important service. But the function of the ministry of the Word is essentially to serve faith. Therefore, the nature of the ministry of the Word in any time and place will be largely determined by what aspect of faith is most significant in that age. In our own day faith is most alive, most meaningful, where it is understood as a gospel hermeneutic of everyday experience resulting in committed Christian praxis. Consequently, the ministry of the Word is essentially a service of that ongoing interpretation. Such service can well take place in the classroom, or the meetings of learned societies, or during the liturgy of the Word.[24] But it will also take place in the street, in the factory, on the farm, in the campus coffee shop, at the bar, after a film, over cocktails in the community room or rectory, at dinner, or wherever Christians come together to subject their real experience to the demands of the Gospel and their traditional or even conventional interpretations of the Gospel to the demands of real life. Christian education is not a ministry whose time has passed; it is a ministry which must recognize itself in new places and transform itself in old places.[25] Because God's revelation came to us as **Word** made flesh, the ministry of the Word will always be the primary ministry of the Church. But because God's Word came to us in the **flesh,** as person and event in our history, we will have to seek new incarnations of that ministry in every age, incarnations that correspond to the faith experience of each new age.

AFTERWORD

My participation in a symposium on Christian Education was definitely that of "one less wise" since, as a biblicist and theologian, I approach the highly professional field of religious education as an interested colleague from outside the field. I learned a great deal about religious education in the two days of the symposium and experienced a gratifying address to my own disciplines from the educational professionals. One highly theological question, which surfaced repeatedly in our discussions and which I did not address in my paper, was that of the relation of religious education as ministry to ordination. In the course of the symposium it became obvious that the cluster of questions centering around the "ordination issue" is crucial, urgent, complex, and, it seemed to me, somewhat confused in its articulation. By means of this "Afterword," I would like to try to put a little order into my own reflections on the question of the relation between the ministry of religious education and ordination, and to provide a framework and incentive for further discussion of the topic.

It seems to me that the question we are considering is multi-dimensional and that distinguishing the major dimensions is a necessary first step toward clarity. Four of these dimensions seemed especially significant in our symposium discussions: the **professional,** which includes questions of credentialing, recognition, and promotion; the **political,** which includes questions of modes of decision-making, job description, and influence; the **economic,** which includes questions of job security, working conditions, and remuneration; and the **sacramental,** in which all ministries, including religious education, must be seen in relation to the culminating expression of Christian identity in the Eucharist. It is important, it seems to me, to clarify for each of these four areas how and why it is de facto related to the ordination issue and then inquire whether it **should** be so related.

The Professional Dimension: Religious education, whatever else it is, is a profession, that is, a service rendered on the basis of acquired competence. In our culture professional competence is certified on the basis of established criteria by a "professional guild" of those in the field, and partially validated in the acceptance of the service by the public to be served—that is, by those who choose to avail themselves of the services of the certified professional. To "practice" effectively in a profession, both the credentialing by the guild and the acceptance by the public served are necessary.

In the Roman Catholic communion an anomalous situation at variance with, if not in outright contradiction to, this cultural arrangement is operative in relation to religious education. Religious education is a **profession** which is exercised as a **ministry.** However, the only ministry officially "credentialed" in the Roman communion seems to be that of the clergy. Consequently, for any other activity, such as religious education, to be accepted as ministry it must be somehow legitimated in the eyes of the public and the Church officials as participation in or extension of the ordained ministry. This creates a frustrating and illogical situation in which the religious educator, although professionally credentialed by an appropriate institution, cannot really exercise her/his profession except in dependence on the clergy who, in most cases, are not professionally competent in the field of religious education. Furthermore, most clergy are considered to have the right to operate as religious educators in any area with which they are connected— parish school, adult education groups, or CCD classes—whether or not they are competent. In other words, the ministerially credentialed religious educators in the Church are those who usually are not professionally qualified, that is, the clergy; and the professionally qualified religious educators are not, for the most part, ministerially credentialed because they are not clergy.

The immediate solution, which was suggested in a number of ways during the symposium, would seem to be to establish in the Church an "ordo" of religious educators, that is, to ordain them for their specific ministry. I am of the theological opinion that this is a poor solution. Ordination is the appointment of a person to a particular ministry, namely that of "ordering," ministering to the apostolic identity, ministry, and mission of the Christian community. To multiply "ordinations" is both to destroy the particular significance of the ordained ministry as community edification by "ordering," and to admit the very principle, now in effect, which desperately needs to be exposed and denied, namely, that there is only one official and public ministry in the Church, that of the ordained. To ordain everyone who legitimately exercises any ministry in the Church is simply to expand the clergy, not to recognize the universal Christian vocation to ministry and the actualization of that vocation in all the different persons who explicitly place the gifts the Spirit has given them at the service of the community. In other words, the task before us is to break up the monopoly of ministry by the ordained, not to increase the numbers who belong to the monopoly.

Because of the historical development (or regression) by which the diverse ministries in the early Church were gradually subsumed into the ordained ministry,[26] the false impression has been created that the Church has and can have only one way of credentialing for ministry: ordination. In fact, this is not true. The ministry of the theologian, for example, even today, is recognized by the conferral of the S.T.L. and/or S.T.D. degrees and the canonical mission to teach. Admittedly, it is only very recently that these degrees have been conferred on non-ordained persons. (One suspects that the full significance of this development escaped the notice of certain ecclesiastical officials when various Pontifical faculties admitted lay persons, including women, to ecclesiastical degree programs!) And they are conferred exclusively by ordained officials. Be this as it may, the fact is that the ministry of the theologian is officially recognized in an appropriate way which is not ordination. The practical consequences of the recognition of the ministry of the theologian, such as respect for the legitimate freedom of investigation of the scholar, are still a matter of contention between theologians and the hierarchy. But the theoretical foundation for eventual, peaceful co-ministry of the two magisteria in the Church is structurally sound.[27]

It is outside my competence to suggest what the appropriate ministerial credentialing of the religious educator should be. But it would seem safe to say that it should come at the close of, and in testimony to, the successful completion of a program of professional ministerial preparation that includes the necessary academic, technical, and spiritual components.

The Political Dimension: Obviously, the political questions involved in the ordination issue closely parallel the professional ones. Again, we are dealing with an historically understandable but very regrettable development in the Church's ministry, namely, that all jurisdictional and administrative powers in the Church came to be seen as an extension of sacramental "powers" conferred by ordination.[28] The result is that decision making, administration, and spheres of influence are not really shared in the Church according to gifts, competencies, and commitments, but are understood in terms of power and are strictly concentrated (occasional collegial or consultative gestures to the contrary notwithstanding) in the hands of the ordained. The Church is organized as a great pyramid composed of smaller pyramids, with a member of the clergy at the peak of each.

The situation is particularly odious to Americans who not only have a cultural preference for participative modes of government but who, in principle, are committed to the proposition that competence is the only legitimate basis for the exercise of leadership in professional spheres. The modern religious educator, technically trained for collaboration in team ministry and theologically convinced that Jesus did not found a divine-right monarchy but a community of equal children of God called to mutual ministry, finds her/himself serving "at the pleasure" of a pastor who probably lacks any professional competence in the field of religious education but who nevertheless sits as the sole authority in the small monarchy of the parish and thus as final judge of who shall educate, how it shall be done, and what content it shall include. Furthermore, his erroneous conviction of absolute authority is backed up in theory and practice by the episcopacy and reinforced by the fact that the pastor usually has final control of the parochial purse.

Again, it seems as if the only solution to this problem is the ordination of religious educators so that they can exercise the only power that really exists in the Church. And again, I am theologically uneasy with this solution. The issue here is a political one, a question of the distribution and exercise of power, not a sacramental or ecclesial one. The error that needs to be dealt with is the very conception of sacramental "power" (problematic in itself) and its political extension (which is both illegitimate and dysfunctional). Ordaining all ministers so that they can participate in an exercise of "power" which ought not to operate in the first place merely compounds the problem. A genuine solution has to be sought in the direction of a theologically-based revisioning of the Church not as a hierarchical power structure controlled by the ordained, but as a participative community carrying out a mutual ministry to itself and to the world, and the implementation of this vision in collegial structures.

The immediate question, of course, is how the present structure caň be so reformed when all power is in the hands of those who stand to lose the most by such reform. This question is not unique to religious education. It is one of the most agonizing and crucial questions facing the Church at large. It seems to me that we must address ourselves to this issue with the wisdom of the serpent and the evangelical idealism of the dove. We must be politically hard-headed enough to admit that groups in power never surrender it willingly even if some members of such a group might renounce the personal exercise of power for gospel reasons. The present exercise of absolute political power by the hierarchy and the clergy of the Church must be broken down by a combination of theological undermining of its theoretical foundations,[29] steady resistance to autocratic exercises of jurisdiction, the repeated assumption and calm exercise of rights which have been denied or violated, the ongoing education of the younger generation in the personal exercise of ecclesial freedom, in short, by every known tactic of peaceful revolution and evolution that can be mustered. But throughout this steady struggle for a different kind of Church we must be sustained by a gospel-based conviction that this is neither rebellion nor disobedience but fidelity to Christ's teaching about the nature of the Kingdom of God and the community which tends toward that Kingdom.

Perhaps the major deterrent to constructive change in the power structure in the Church is the fact that most Catholics (perhaps including some religious educators) are convinced that the present structure is "willed by Christ" and therefore that they are powerless within it unless they are ordained. Theologians and religious educators have a special role to play in dissipating this conviction. It will certainly not be dissipated by the tacit acceptance of it implied in seeking the ordination of all ministers so that they can participate in power as it is defined and exercised in the present structure.

The Economic Dimension: It seems clear enough that, if the professional and political issues of the ministerial situation of the religious educator were rectified, the economic issues could be handled fairly easily. However, in the meantime, the semi-credentialed (i.e., professionally but not ministerially) and politically disenfranchised religious educator must deal with the fact that she or he is totally without economic leverage in the ecclesiastical structure. Not only does this make for an often unbearable financial insecurity, especially for those supporting families, but it puts the religious educators in a highly compromised position professionally. The person totally dependent for his or her job on the pastor can ill afford to put professional convictions ahead of the latter's will. It is not only financial insecurity, poor pay, and frustration, but also the violation of professional integrity and personal dignity that drive many competent religious educators out of this ministry.

As I have tried to suggest, the long-range solution to the economic problems of this ministry as well as others lies in a renewed Church order. Probably the only immediate relief lies in the direction suggested by Thomas Groome during the symposium, namely, some effective form of unionization that would allow for collective bargaining. This type of suggestion meets with instinctive resistance in the heart of the committed minister, seeming to smack of the commercialization of the Word of God. But the issue here is economic justice and professional integrity, and the only protection of rights in these spheres, short of a truly evangelical community structure (which is still in the future), is collective influence. There is nothing venal or crass about the protection of one's rights. Indeed, in some cases, for instance, that of a person with financial dependents or that of a person whose acceptance of injustice undermines the rights of others, the protection of one's economic rights is an obligation in justice. Furthermore, the establishing of a certain **economic** equality and mutual dependence between the religious educator as professional and her or his ecclesiastical employer could help move the latter toward an understanding that the **ministry** of the religious educator is equal to and in mutuality with his own ministry. Money is, unfortunately, a reality principle of unusual persuasion in our Church! What the officials must pay for they must take seriously, however much we might wish that it were vice versa. In other words, the struggle for economic justice is not simply the private struggle of the religious educator but a real contribution to a new vision of full-time ministry in the Church as a calling open to all Christians and not solely to those who are male, celibate, and called to the ministry of community order.

The Sacramental Dimension: The only really theological argument for the ordination of religious educators has to do with the real relation of all ministry to the culminating expression of Christian identity in the celebration of the Eucharist and the frustration of many non-ordained ministers at being unable to celebrate Eucharist (and other Sacraments) with those to whom they minister—since at the present time in the Roman Catholic community it is official teaching that no Eucharistic liturgy may legitimately and validly be celebrated unless an ordained priest is presiding. This last statement needs to be "unpacked" if we are to understand the present pastoral problem.

As is well known, the New Testament does not tell us who presided at Eucharist in the earliest Church. Nor does the New Testament refer to any group of ordained ministers who had special cultic functions.[30] Finally, the New Testament makes no reference to Christian priests at all. Consequently, the origins of the reasons for the present arrangement which ties Eucharistic celebration to the physical presence of an ordained minister in an absolute way must be looked for in post-apostolic developments.[31] How did this arrangement develop?

First, the emergence of a group of church leaders who had administrative, leadership, and unifying functions in the community begins in the New Testament period itself[32] and, in at least some locations, was relatively well developed by the early second century.[33] Since the Eucharist is the ultimate celebration of the unity of the faithful in Christ it is not surprising that at an early date it became customary in some locations (such as the churches to whom Ignatius wrote) for the persons charged with the ministry of unity to preside at the community's Eucharist.[34] Because the Eucharist was also the primary proclamation of the Word of Salvation within the Church, prophets were also recognized as natural presidents of the Eucharist.[35] In house celebrations the head of the Christian house church probably presided. At any rate, it seems that fairly early in the Church's history the role of presiding at Eucharist came to be considered a special community function and certain people were designated to carry it out. It seems doubtful, however, that in the earliest communities anyone was ordained for this task exclusively or even primarily. Rather, those who held certain positions of community leadership, for which they were ordained, were recognized as the appropriate leaders of the Eucharistic assembly. This restriction of Eucharistic presidency undoubtedly also accomplished the important subsidiary function of insuring that the leaders of Eucharistic worship were liturgically and theologically competent for this important ministry.

Secondly, as the Eucharistic celebration gradually came to be understood as a sacrifice (early second century?),[36] the view emerged that it must be performed by an authorized "priest." This also, of course, suggested that, at least insofar as the Eucharist was a sacrifice, it really was done **only** by the priest and merely attended or witnessed by the people, even if, insofar as it was a covenant meal, it was the work of the Christian community as a whole.

Thirdly, as the theology of Eucharistic transformation hardened into a quite materialistic, quasi-magical, theory of transubstantiation, it came to be thought that the act of "confection" could be performed only by someone possessed of miraculous power, a power thought to be conferred by ordination. This logically entailed, all communitarian rhetoric to the contrary notwithstanding, that the ordained confecter was the sole necessary and sufficient human agent in the celebration of Eucharist.[37] With this development we have arrived at the Tridentine position with which we began: no valid Eucharist is possible unless it is done by an ordained priest.

The problem we face today is, in origin, a pastoral one. Many Christians are far more conscious today of the real meaning of the Eucharist, not as a rite they must attend in order to give infinite glory to God, nor as a source of infinite grace for themselves and others, but as the most adequate expression of their gratitude-filled experience of who they are as Christians. Eucharist is the ultimate giving of thanks for and celebration of their salvific unity in Christ and with Christ. A certain spiritual authenticity has replaced the quasi-magical **ex opere operato** mentality of pre-Conciliar days and it is therefore no longer a matter of indifference when, where, and with whom one celebrates Eucharist. Certain experiences, such as important gatherings of a religious community, experiences of long-awaited reconciliation in families, shared prayer experiences, experiences of profound healing, the reaching of certain personal

and communal milestones, the culmination of sacramental preparation, etc., lead naturally to Eucharist. But often, perhaps most of
the time, this natural desire for Eucharist is frustrated because there
is no ordained minister available, or those who are available are
either unsuitable or simply foreigners to the human event which is
being brought to Eucharistic expression. What are the options in
such a case?

One option is for the group to celebrate a non-Eucharistic
liturgy. Efforts to convince people that this is an excellent solution
have simply not worked, and I am tempted to think that, at least
among those whom I know to be experiencing this type of frustration, this is not due to any magical mentality regarding the
Eucharist. It is a profound Christian instinct for the special significance of the meal that Jesus left us.

The second option is for the group to bring in a priest who is
not part of the reality being brought to Eucharistic expression and
to plan the celebration so as to insert the priest as unobtrusively as
possible at the "crucial" points. This is not only demeaning for the
priest, but it is also very unsatisfactory for the community which is,
in effect, "celebrating around" a priest—who, if necessary, is yet an
impediment to an integral community experience. Theologically, it
tends to lead back toward a highly magical interpretation of priesthood as a source of numinous "power" for the saying of magic
formulas.

Or, as happens most often, the group simply lives with the
frustration of being unable to celebrate, unable to do that which
Jesus asked and empowered us to do in memory of him. As this
happens more and more frequently, we run the risk of becoming a
less and less Eucharistic people because the Eucharist which we
can celebrate is not the one which is expressive of the most significant moments of thanks in our lives, and the moments of deepest
thanksgiving cannot be expressed Eucharistically.

It is this pastoral impasse that leads to the statement we hear
ever more frequently among the non-ordained in all kinds of
ministries: "I wish I could be ordained just so that I could celebrate
Eucharist with the people to whom I minister." And it is this
impasse which suggests to me that we must reexamine the
theological foundations of the current practice which requires an
ordained priest as president of every Eucharist and perhaps explore
the possibility of some modification of this discipline.[38]

Let us start with the question of "power." It is at least a defensible theological position that ordination, however late scholasticism eventually came to understand it, does not confer any special "power" on the ordained, nor is any "power" (as distinct from right to exercise the power), other than that of the Spirit of Christ given to the Christian by baptism, necessary for or operative in the celebration of Eucharist. "Every Christian has the power to do whatever the Church is responsible to do."[39] The true celebrant of the Eucharist is the apostolic community, that is, the community of baptized disciples of Jesus. Whatever the presence of the priest contributes, it is not a special personal power to transubstantiate without which Eucharist does not "work." What ordination does do, it seems, is designate the minister who alone has the right to preside legitimately at Christian Eucharist. And the Church does have the right to organize its ministries in this way.

Secondly, let us look at the question of sacrifice and the need for a "priest." The sacrifice in which we participate in Eucharist is that which has been offered once and for all by the only priest of the Christian community, Jesus Christ. By baptism we participate in that eternal priesthood. The ordained Christian symbolizes and even represents to the community its participation in the priesthood of Christ, but he does not bring to the celebration some kind of personal and special priesthood apart from the priesthood of Christ shared by all his members which is necessary for this sacrifice to take place.[40] It is the priesthood of Christ which alone is necessary and sufficient for this sacrifice, and it is their baptismal participation in his priesthood which enables the community, including its ordained members, to participate as subjects in his sacrifice.

This leaves only one real reason why the presence and leadership of the ordained are required for the celebration of Eucharist. This reason has both theological and ecclesiastical aspects. Theologically, the ordained minister has been incorporated in a special way into the apostolic ministry. Now, by "apostolic ministry" we must not understand "the only ministry in the Church that is apostolic," for no ministry is genuine unless it is apostolic. But those in "orders" in the Church have, as their special ministry, to symbolize and to serve the apostolicity and the unity of the whole Church. The community of believers, whether local or universal, can celebrate Eucharist only because and to the extent that that community is the apostolic community, the community of believers in Jesus Christ united with him in the Body of the Church. The presence and leadership of the ordained minister both symbolize and certify the apostolicity of the celebrating community.

Ecclesiastically, the requirement of the presidency of the ordained is a way of ensuring, to the degree possible (and obviously it is not always possible!), that the president of the assembly is liturgically competent.

In the light of the foregoing I would raise, very tentatively, a suggestion concerning the present pastoral impasse. We know, as a leadership ministry emerged in the early Church and Eucharistic presidency came to be seen as an appropriate function of that ministry, that only the Bishop was considered the legitimate president.[41] However, as size of local congregations and other factors made a single celebration with the Bishop presiding impractical, he delegated the function of presidency to his colleagues, the presbyters (whence, incidentally, our term "priests"). My question is, are we not in a similar situation today? Is it not the case that practical considerations make the celebration of every Eucharist with the ordained minister a virtual impossibility? Could not the real purposes of restricting Eucharistic presidency to the ordained be accomplished by the prudent delegation of this function to some of the ordained minister's non-ordained colleagues who he knows are liturgically competent and who actually do embody in their ministerial identity and service the apostolicity of the local group? What the priest would be doing, in effect, would be declaring "official" or "public" the symbolizing role which those ministers already exercise charismatically, thus maintaining the real union of this role with the apostolic ministry of "order" and at the same time exercising "quality control" of the ministry of Eucharistic leadership.

Who might some of these "special presidents" of Eucharistic celebration be? Among those who come readily to mind are religious superiors or those members of the local religious communities who are the de facto spiritual leaders of their respective groups: hospital and prison ministers; home ministers to shut-ins; campus ministers; trained religious educators; and certain known and experienced spiritual directors.

Again the question could be asked, "Why not simply ordain these ministers?" And again, my answer is that the ordained ministry has a particular function in the Church, namely, that of leadership with its special service to the apostolicity, unity, and mission of the community. These other ministers do not assume that particular responsibility in the local or universal Church, even though they may represent that ministry in some particular respect and for some particular occasion in some subdivision of the local church. The primary ministerial problem in the contemporary Church is that the entire wide spectrum of ministries which arose in the New Testament church has been subsumed and monopolized by the ordained ministry. The solution to this problem lies in the direction of restoring the plurality and diversity of ministries in the Church, which implies regaining the realization that ordained ministry is one important, but limited, ministry and that it is not the source or legitimator of the others. This necessary restructuring of ministry in the Church cannot be accomplished by ordaining all who minister. This might help in the short range with some practical personnel problems, but it would only reaffirm the error we are trying to correct, namely, that to be a genuine and legitimate minister in the Church we must be ordained and that only the ordained are real ministers. In short, the ordained ministry needs to be contained, not expanded, if other ministries are to emerge fully.

My expression of some of these ideas at the symposium occasioned considerable lively discussion and debate. I hope their expression here, which I trust is a little more clear and coherent, will give rise to continued discussion in wider circles.

NOTES

1. I am using "Christian education" in its broadest sense to include not only classroom instruction but all forms of witness to the Gospel including evangelization, preaching, teaching, and prophecy, however and wherever and by whomever they are done, provided that the witness is authentically apostolic, i.e., that it stands within the tradition coming from the apostles.

2. No pretension to a definition of the Church is intended by this statement. The difficulty of defining the Church was well demonstrated by Richard P. McBrien in **Church: The Continuing Quest** (New York: Paulist

Press, Newman Press, 1970). I merely want to insist that mission is constitutive of the Church.

3. The more traditional formula, "proclaiming the coming of the Kingdom of God," is being avoided, not only out of deference to the sensibilities of women and peoples emerging from colonial situations who find patriarchal and dominative language offensive, but also because it tends to suggest a static understanding of the salvation proclaimed by Jesus as a place or state of affairs or even a community ruled by God rather than as the **action** of God. On this point see J. D. Crossan, **In Parables: The Challenge of the Historical Jesus** (New York: Harper & Row, 1973), p. 23; N. Perrin, **Rediscovering the Teaching of Jesus** (New York: Harper & Row, 1976 [orig. publ. 1967]), pp. 54-60.

4. Although this passage occurs in the disputed appendix to Mark's gospel it is a valuable witness to the first century Church's understanding of the mission received by the first disciples from the risen Jesus.

5. The seeming lack in the Fourth Gospel of a commission to preach the Word is more apparent than real. In John 20:22-23 the glorified Jesus shares with his disciples his own mission of taking away the sin of the world (cf. John 1:29), which he accomplished precisely by bearing witness to the truth (John 18:37).

6. That no rigid distinction, much less opposition, between ministers of the Word and ministers to the material needs of the community is implied by this passage is clear from what follows. The Seven actually constitute the first leadership collegium of the Hellenist Christian community (see R. E. Brown, **Priest and Bishop: Biblical Reflections** [New York: Paulist Press, 1970], pp. 56-57) and at least two of them, Stephen (Acts 6:8-10) and Philip (Acts 8:5-6, 26-40), are outstanding ministers of the Word. The point of the passage is the primacy of the claim of ministry of the Word upon the one called to it.

7. The Greek text with English translation is available in **The Apostolic Fathers,** trans. K. Lake, Loeb Classical Library (Cambridge, Mass.: Harvard University Press, 1970), I, 303-333. For a fluent English translation with a helpful introduction see **Early Christian Fathers,** trans. and ed. C. C. Richardson and collaborators (New York: Macmillan, 1970), pp. 161-179.

8. **Didache** 15:1-2; see also 10:7, 11:1-4.

9. **Didache** 13:1-7. It is interesting in this regard to note that the verb translated as "minister" is λειτουργέω, and that prophets are the only ministers who are permitted to offer Eucharist "in their own way," i.e., without being bound to the prescribed texts (cf. 10:7).

10. I have translated ἡ βασιλεία τοῦ Θεοῦ in accord with the remarks in note 3 above.

11. For an excellent and detailed treatment of the subject of the ministry of the Word see Bernard J. Cooke, **Ministry to Word and Sacraments** (Philadelphia: Fortress, 1976), pp. 219-340.

12. The most thorough exploration of the nature and dynamics of faith in the New Testament is the Fourth Gospel. The interested reader will find a relatively extensive bibliography on faith in the Gospel of John in my article "Symbolism and the Sacramental Principle in the Fourth Gospel,"

Segni e Sacramenti nel Vangelo di Giovanni, edit. P.-R. Tragan [Studia Anselmiana: Sacramentum 3] (Roma: Editrice Anselmiana, 1977), p. 227, n. 15.

13. See Cooke, pp. 219-225.

14. It is interesting to note that the editors of the **New Catholic Encyclopedia** considered it necessary to update the article "Faith" by C. H. Pickar (which appeared in Vol. V, 792-796, in 1967), with a new article by J. Fichtner, "Faith, Act of," **NCE,** Vol. XVII [Supplement: Change in the Church] (Washington, D.C./New York: Publishers Guild, Inc., in association with McGraw-Hill, 1979), 224-225. The opening sentences of the two articles are subtly indicative of the change in understanding. The 1967 article defines faith as "belief in God and acceptance of His revelation as true" (p. 792), and the 1979 article defines faith as "the name for the response to revelation" (p. 224). The former definition is still largely controlled by the First Vatican Council's definition of faith as intellectual assent to the truths of revelation on the authority of God revealing (cf. Denz. 1789), whereas the latter reflects the more wholistic approach to the subject characteristic of contemporary theology.

15. This is most apparent in Paul's frequent descriptions of his understanding of his own vocation (e.g., Rom. 1:1,9; 1 Cor. 1:1; 2 Cor. 1:1, 3:5-6, 4:3-7, etc.).

16. See note 14 above for references.

17. The Council recognized the singular importance for both the understanding and the practice of faith in the new context in which faith is situated today, a context of atheism, secularism, and religious pluralism (**Gaudium et Spes,** #19-21).

18. The study by Andrew M. Greeley and Peter H. Rossi, **The Education of Catholic Americans** (New York: Anchor Books, 1968), caused a veritable storm of conflicting interpretations and conclusions about the effectiveness of Catholic school education. The study by Andrew M. Greeley, William C. McCready, and Kathleen McCourt, **Catholic Schools in a Declining Church** (Kansas City: Sheed & Ward, 1976), indicates that considerably more optimism about the Catholic school system is warranted than present Church policy expresses.

19. A particularly interesting example of the complexity of the concept of faith is the recent special issue of **Theological Studies** 39 (Dec. 1978), entitled **Faith in the Contemporary World** and produced by the faculty of the Jesuit School of Theology at Berkeley.

20. The Greeley-McCready-McCourt study (see note 18 above) suggests that there might be a real gap between the facts about the effectiveness of Catholic education and the perception of effectiveness by many observers, including some educators themselves.

21. By listing these groups together I do not intend to suggest either that they are equally adequate as faith contexts or that the interpretation and use of the Scriptures in all of these groups is equally good or even minimally accurate. In many groups of these types, fundamentalism, particularism, excessive individualism, unsound political biases, and other disturbing influences seriously undermine their use of the Scriptures.

What I wish to point to in these groups is simply the **role** assigned to Scripture by all of them. Whether they use the Word well or badly they all attempt to enlighten concrete experience by means of the Scriptures and, to some extent, to enlighten the Scriptures by experience. It is this dialectic between Word and life experience implying an understanding of faith as hermeneutic of concrete everyday experience which I find significant. It is the pedagogical model of praxis-theory-praxis which such an under-standing of faith demands, not the adequacy of the use of the model in any particular group, which is an important indicator to me of the way in which Christian education as ministry of the Word could be usefully understood today.

22. Fundamentally, this is precisely the way contemporary theology is being done by its most creative practitioners, as McBrien points out in his discussion of the "method of correlation." (**Church: The Continuing Quest**, pp. 12-21.)

23. A good example of serious academic Scripture study done from a starting point in praxis is Phyllis Trible's **God and the Rhetoric of Sexuality** (Philadelphia: Fortress, 1978). Some interesting examples of a class analysis approach to biblical texts as well as reflections on the use of such methods can be found in **The Bible and Liberation: Political and Social Hermeneutics,** coord. by N. D. Gottwald (Berkeley: Radical Religion, 1976). Walter Wink, in **The Bible in Human Transformation** (Philadelphia: Fortress, 1973), explains and illustrates a type of communal exegesis which begins in psycho-social experience. Perhaps the best known and most accessible, sustained effort to do practical theology from a liberation per-spective is the series entitled "A Theology for Artisans of a New Human-ity" by Juan L. Segundo (Maryknoll, N.Y.: Orbis).

24. Very interesting reflections on more effective praxis-theory-praxis models of theological education are coming from the growing numbers of professionals in the area of theological field education. Several interesting articles on this subject appear in a special issue of **Theological Education** 11 (Summer 1975), entitled **Theological Field Education for Ministry.**

In 1979 a working group on "Biblical Hermeneutics and Liberation Theology" was originated by members of The Society for Biblical Litera-ture, the world's largest professional association of biblical scholars. This group has set a five-year goal of "contributing toward an indigenous liberation theology for our time and society" (from a memorandum to members dated April 1979).

25. I read, after the 1979 Symposium, two articles by Thomas H. Groome: "Christian Education: A Task of Present Dialectical Hermeneu-tics," **The Living Light** 14 (Fall 1977): 408-423, and "Christian Education for Freedom: A 'Shared Praxis' Approach," in **Foundations of Religious Education,** ed. P. O'Hare (New York: Paulist, 1978), pp. 8-39, which dem-onstrate that such transformation is actually taking place. In these articles Groome describes the actual practice, within the classroom setting, of the type of religious education about which I am theorizing.

26. For a good historical overview of this development see B. J. Cooke, "Introduction," **Ministry to Word and Sacraments,** pp. 1-30.

27. An important discussion of the relation between the pastoral and

theological magisteria is the 1976 presidential address of A. Dulles to the Catholic Theological Society of America entitled, "The Theologian and the Magisterium," **Proceedings of the Thirty-First Annual Convention,** vol. 31, ed. L. Salm (CTSA: 1976), 235-246.

28. Cooke, in **Ministry to Word and Sacraments,** pp. 516-520, raises the question of whether the category of jurisdictional authority can be legitimately applied in the Christian community and answers in the negative.

29. The writings of such theologically diverse authors as K. Rahner, **The Shape of the Church to Come** (New York: Seabury, 1972); J. L. McKenzie, **Authority in the Church** (New York: Doubleday, 1971); H. Küng, **Infallible? An Inquiry,** trans. E. Mosbacher (London: Collins, 1971); and A. Dulles, **Models of the Church** (New York: Doubleday, 1974), as well as the ecumenical statements of the Anglican-Roman Catholic International Commission, "Authority in the Church" (Venice: 1976) and of the Lutheran-Roman Catholic Dialogue, **Papal Primacy and the Universal Church,** ed. P. C. Empie and T. A. Murphy (Minneapolis: Augsburg, 1974) are contributing to this rethinking of ecclesial authority.

30. For good treatments of the New Testament material on ministry see R. E. Brown, **Priest and Bishop: Biblical Reflections,** and A. Lemaire, **Ministry in the Church,** trans. C. W. Danes (London: SPCK, 1977), pp. 3-41.

31. Brown, in **Priest and Bishop,** pp. 42-43, points out that, at least in some churches, e.g., those addressed by Ignatius of Antioch (d. 107?), (see Smyrneans 8:1), the role of presiding at Eucharist had been restricted to the bishop or a presbyter designated by him by the end of the first century.

32. See 1 Tim. 3:1-7; Titus 1:7-9; 1 Pet. 5:1-5; Phil. 1:1; Eph. 4:11.

33. Our clearest evidence of this is the letters of Ignatius of Antioch but there is also some evidence in 1 Clement 42:4-5; 44:1-6 (c. 96 A.D.), and in the **Didache** 13:1-7; 15:1-2 (second century).

34. That the primary task of the established official ministry in the Church was the edification of the Church in unity is clear already in Eph. 4:11-14, and Ignatius' insistence on the importance of the bishop's role is based on his concept of the bishop as the visible focus and guarantee of the unity of the church (e.g., Magnesians 7; Philadelphians 1-4; Smyrneans 8).

35. See **Didache** 10:7.

36. See Brown, **Priest and Bishop,** pp. 18-19.

37. An excellent presentation of the development of the theology of confection from its beginnings shortly after the Pauline period to the post-Tridentine period and of the theological emphases and implications of this theology is available in J. M. Powers' article, "Eucharist: Symbol of Freedom and Community," **Christian Spirituality in the United States, Independence and Interdependence,** ed. F. A. Eigo (Villanova: University Press, 1978), pp. 187-209.

38. A recent abstract "The Eucharist Today," **Theology Digest** 25 (Spring 1977): 24-31, reported the position of a number of highly reputable theologians (H. Küng, E. Schillebeeckx, W. Kasper, W. Breuning, K. Rahner) on the question of whether a valid Eucharist could be celebrated by an unordained Christian in emergency circumstances if no priest were

available. The consensus was in the affirmative. This suggests to me that we might need to recognize sacramental "emergency" in situations other than the proverbial "desert island." It also argues strongly against the notion of "power" as the priest's necessary contribution to Eucharist.

39. I borrow this clear and precise sentence from R. McBrien who used it in one of his interventions at the symposium.

40. It is difficult to assign any clear theological content to the repeated official affirmations that the priesthood of the ordained is somehow "essentially different" from that of the non-ordained (see, e.g., **Lumen Gentium** 2:#10). Since there is only one priesthood that has Christian significance, namely, that of Christ, the apparent implication of an essential difference between the priesthood of the ordained and unordained would seem to be that one or the other does not participate in the Christian priesthood. One of the better attempts to explain the "two priesthoods" is the article of A. Vanhoye, "Sacerdoce commun et sacerdoce ministériel: distinction et rapports," **Nouvelle revue theologique** 97 (Mar. 1975):193-207.

H. Küng in **Why Priests? A Proposal for a New Church Ministry,** trans. R. C. Collins (New York: Doubleday, 1972), pp. 41-42, makes the useful suggestion that we drop the term "priest" as a designation of a particular ministry in the Church and designate ordained ministers by function. I also recommend a very interesting and persuasive position paper on this same subject by D. Aschbeck, "The Ordained Ministerial Presbyterate: A Position Paper," **Schola** 1 (1978):61-78.

41. See Brown, **Priest and Bishop,** p. 42.

QUESTIONS FOR DISCUSSION

1) Schneiders equates "Christian education" with the "ministry of the Word." She later suggests that the very question of the issue of the relationship of ministry **and** education—rather than the issue of the ministry **of** education—is indicative of the present "ministerial malaise." Does she thereby stand in agreement with Butler's contention that "ministry is the umbrella term under which true Christian education falls"? Is this, in your view, an adequate way of conceptualizing the relationship?

2) The ministry of the Word functions to evoke, sustain, nurture, and challenge faith. Thus, one's understanding of faith is key to the practice of ministry. Where would you locate yourself in Schneiders' description of the differing understandings of faith from the first century (conversion of adults), to the second and third centuries (demonstration of the validity of Christianity), to the Counter-Reformation (intellectual assent to propositions), to postwar (personal commitment to Christ) and contemporary (an interpretive key for looking at reality in the light of the Gospel, impelling one toward action in faith)?

3) How has membership in any of the small grassroots communities to which Schneiders refers influenced your understanding and practice of faith? What difference has it made in your ministry?

4) Schneiders argues that faith is most alive and meaningful when it is regarded as a "gospel hermeneutic of everyday experience resulting in committed Christian praxis." What, in your mind, is a "gospel hermeneutic"? Does such language give proper acknowledgment to the function of the Hebrew Scriptures in Christian life?

5) During the symposium itself, the question of the ordination of women surfaced repeatedly among participants and panelists. Why, in your opinion, has this issue become so significant for people involved in education and ministry? What might the

experience of Protestant denominations contribute to analysis of
the issue of ordination?

6) Schneiders notes the manner by which the ministry of the
theologian is officially recognized. No comparable way of be-
stowing credentials presently exists for religious educators.
Should this be done? If so, how?

7) On what basis does Schneiders argue that ordination as a means
of obtaining professional credentials or political power is not
theologically sound? Evaluate her suggestion that the present
pastoral impasse, in which experiences that might well culmi-
nate in the Eucharist are frustrated because there is no available
or suitable ordained minister, might be solved by prudent delegation to non-ordained, liturgically competent and ministerially
qualified persons.

Ministry in Education
from a Pastoral-Theological Perspective
by Virgil P. Elizondo

AUTOBIOGRAPHICAL STATEMENT

I was born and raised in San Antonio, Texas, in an entirely Spanish-speaking neighborhood. It was not until I went to school that I started to learn English—after having failed the first grade because I had no idea what the teachers were speaking about. As far back as I can remember, I have many vivid memories of my parents' involvement in various social and political affairs that would help our Mexican American people.

After finishing high school with honors, I went on to finish a degree in chemistry and mathematics, also with honors, as I was interested in becoming a scientist and devoting my time to scientific research. However, as my college years progressed, I decided that it was not in the laboratories that I wanted to spend my life, but in direct contact with people. It was with this in mind that I decided to go to a seminary to become a priest.

I did my seminary training in Assumption Seminary in San Antonio, Texas, and was ordained a priest for the diocese of San Antonio in 1963. My first assignment was in a small inner-city parish of San Antonio where I met all kinds of people within my first weeks of ordination. From there I was sent to a tri-lingual country parish where the common languages were German, Polish, and Spanish. This was a very exciting assignment, and I quickly became aware of the unsuspected cultural agendas which are often active but never verbalized or discussed.

In 1967 I was appointed archdiocesan director of religious education. Since I had no background in this field, I asked for permission to take a year off to prepare myself. I went to the East Asian Pastoral Institute in Manila, where I studied under such great men as Fathers Alfonso Nebreda and Johannes Hofinger. It was a great experience to live and study and pray in the same household with people of twenty-nine different nationalities. I have no doubts that this year in Asia was one of the most exciting and growth-filled experiences of my life. It was during this year that I wrote my first book, **The Human Quest, A Search for Meaning through Life and Death.**

After returning to San Antonio, I was asked to be in charge of updating the seminary curriculum, in accordance with Vatican II. Thus, I continued as director of religious education and as dean of studies of our major seminary. The years of the Conciliar reform were both exciting and painful. Yet there was no doubt that we were part of a Church that was very much alive.

In 1971, I was asked by the bishops of Texas to become director of what was to become the Mexican American Cultural Center. At the time that I was asked to be director of the Center, it had no budget whatsoever, no location, no personnel, and not even a name. I was to be director of an idea that did not yet exist. But it was an exciting assignment and filled with faith in God. I was crazy enough to accept and to begin the work of what is today the Mexican American Cultural Center. I might add that there was no salary or expense account attached to this assignment: it was up to me to find them. The risk was tremendous, yet the last nine years have been the most exciting years of my life. In many ways, it has been a part of an ongoing miracle in process. Thousands of people have come through our Center and have been totally transformed in the experience of our workshops. Our staff has grown from zero to thirty, and our budget has grown from zero to somewhere in the millions. We still have no guaranteed income, but the money manages to come each year.

Since then, I have published my second book, **Christianity and Culture,** and also have had numerous periodical articles published internationally. I have also directed two national television programs and participated in two others. I have helped produce television programs in Europe dealing with questions of the Spanish-speaking in the United States, in addition to participating in numerous committees, workshops, and courses throughout the world.

From 1976-77 I went to the Institut Catholique in Paris to complete work on my doctoral dissertation in theology. The thesis, entitled **Metissage, Violence Culturelle, Annonce de L'Evangile,** was defended in Paris in 1978 and was accorded the highest honors. In 1979 I was awarded an honorary Doctorate of Humanities by Siena Heights College in Adrian, Michigan.

I suspect the most exciting experience during this time was participation in the Latin American meetings of Medellin in 1968 and of Puebla in 1979. I was also elected to serve on the editorial board of **Concilium** and have enjoyed working shoulder-to-shoulder with those who are in many ways the backbone and the brains of Vatican II.

Today I find that the most exciting thing happening in the Church is the reintroduction of a theological method that does not come from on high but rather takes as its point of departure the living faith of the particular faith community. I realize that this method is not understood or appreciated in the Western world; nevertheless, I am convinced that it is one of the most exciting rediscoveries in the universal Church. I find that doing theology with the grassroots believing community is one of the most rewarding experiences possible. Christ and the Church really come alive when the believing community begins together to seek out the meaning of its faith experience so as to communicate it to others in a meaningful way. The theology that comes out of such reflections far surpasses what I have read in the best of theological books and journals of recent times by the best of authors. It is to this work of theologizing with the people and out of their experience that our own Mexican American Cultural Center is committed in order to proclaim the Gospel effectively in today's world.

Virgil P. Elizondo

INTRODUCTORY REMARKS[1]

The Church has always seen itself as teacher: "Go forth and make disciples of all the nations . . . teaching them. . . ." (Matt. 28:18-20). Throughout the ages, the Church has seen its mission as one of teaching, ruling, and sanctifying. Yet the understanding of this triple mission has varied greatly from age to age and from region to region depending on the way people have envisioned

Christ, Church, and World. The implicit anthropology of a given period will influence the way people conceive of Church and Christ; and our conception of Christ will either be the ultimate affirmation of the make-up of the Church and the world or it will be the critical question which will urge both Church and world into bold and radical transformation. Thus, a dynamic interrelationship and, at times, a tension exist among the anthropology, ecclesiology, and christology functioning at a given point and place.

All baptized Christians are called upon to share in some way in the threefold mission of teaching, ruling, and sanctifying. But precisely how, and to what extent, they will actually prepare for and participate in this mission will depend on their working concepts of Christ-Church-World.

For the sake of this presentation, I will use the terms **ministry** and **education** in their simple dictionary meanings. Thus ministry means a service or function that is often associated with religion which one performs for another. Education, in a literate society such as ours, means a formal course of study of some sort or another. Education always has a goal; and in view of that goal, a program of studies is elaborated.

Ministry and education in the Church will be determined by the interplay among christology-ecclesiology-anthropology. During my own personal life as a priest (ordained in 1963), I have experienced a fascinating evolution which, in effect, has been a total transformation of the way in which the Church has understood itself, its founder, its members, and its mission. In order to demonstrate this ecclesiological process of growth, I propose to examine the basic models and images which have prevailed in recent times, subdividing them into three main periods: (1) pre-Vatican II; (2) Vatican II; and finally, (3) John Paul II and Puebla. I will try to show how the basic understanding of anthropology, ecclesiology, and christology determines the concepts of ministry and education in today's world.[2] I will seek to show that, as the Church continues to delve deeper both into the mystery of Christ and into the mystery of humanity, it will consistently discover new and deeper aspects of its mission. Furthermore, I will highlight how new aspects of christology will lead both to new aspects of ecclesiology and to new aspects of anthropology.

I. PRE-VATICAN II

A. Anthropology

Generally speaking, this period may be characterized as an era in which inequality was accepted as the ordinary way of life. For the most part, the classist-racist vision of men[3] of Western Europe and America had gone unchallenged. People generally accepted and adjusted to the reality of living in an unequal society. People repudiated Marxism because of its atheism, but failed to acknowledge that one of the causes of atheism was certainly the failure of Christians to work for the classless society wherein all could experience the universal community of the children of God (**Gaudium et Spes** #19).

During this time, clergy and religious provided the services offered by the Church; ordination or reception of vows was considered as adequate preparation for almost any task the Church wanted to assign. Professionalism, although evident in some areas, was generally not considered as essential for Church work. The priests ran the parish as effectively administered "sacramental factories," the sisters ran the schools and hospitals, and the laity helped out wherever they could in organizations such as St. Vincent de Paul, Legion of Mary, and CCD.

In this model, the hierarchical Church alone controlled knowledge; the "teaching" Church alone knew what it meant to be Catholic; it alone could interpret the faith; it alone was concerned with its transmission. Indeed, the Church seemed to belong chiefly to the clergy and religious and only secondly to the laity, who merely prayed and helped in the mission of the hierarchy. Their unique task was to pray, pay, and obey.

A similar division existed in the world order. It was commonly accepted that people and persons were divided by nature itself into superior and inferior beings. Even though democracy supposedly functioned in some of the nations of the world, various types of hierarchies functioned nevertheless within each nation and within the world as a whole.

B. Ecclesiology

Because the Church shared the classist and racist world view, it manifested many of those characteristics. The Church saw itself as the **societas perfecta,** with a well-defined hierarchy, body of knowledge, sacred rites, and unbending norms. Everyone had his or her place in the pyramidal structure of the Church. One simply has to recall the precision with which the master of ceremonies of a liturgical procession would line everybody up according to ecclesiastical rank. These rankings vividly illustrated the understanding of the Church as an absolute monarchy, with the Pope at the top and the laity at the bottom.[4] Cardinals, bishops, priests, and religious formed the intermediate classes.

On the basis of the models of the day, ministry and education were quite simple. The subject matter was clearly determined; one had merely to fill the requirements. Ordination, episcopal consecration, or religious profession were the unquestioned credentials that one was ready for ministry in the Church.

During this period, the education of the future minister took place strictly in the seminary classroom, and formation was an initiation into an "other-world" spirituality. The ministers were to be separated from anything worldly so that they would dedicate themselves to the things of God: they were to be mediators between God and man. Therefore, degrees were not necessary and most of the seminaries had not even contemplated accreditation.

Serious programs of theology at the academic level were generally unheard of, since theology was the domain of the seminary. For the rest, courses in religion sufficed. In any case, reliance on the magisterium made the Church an unquestioned teacher; if in doubt, one accepted the teaching "on faith."

In short, this was the period of oppressive domination. The clergy and religious had claimed for themselves the prerogative of every baptized Christian: ministry in accordance with one's charisms to the needs of the community and the world. The laity were merely allowed to help in the apostolate of the hierarchy, and were thereby condemned to a perpetual inferiority, a second-class citizenship in the Church. Only the clergy had the power to minister and teach religion; the only model of sanctity was that of religious life.

C. Christology

Anthropology and ecclesiology in many ways establish the focus through which the Church views Christ.

As might already be suspected from the anthropology and ecclesiology of this period, its christology emphasized the divinity, the pre-existence, the power, the eternal priesthood, and the sanctity of Christ to such a degree that his humanity was greatly eclipsed. He was portrayed almost exclusively as a Christ of power, seated at the right hand of the Father, who would come to judge the living and the dead. Jesus in turn shared this absolute power of judgment with the hierarchy (collectively the **alter Christus**) and with established authority. The higher up one went in power, the more he (always **he**) was presumed to share in the absolute power of Christ himself.[5] This view of Christ legitimized both the structures of the Church and of society.

As society developed and evolved, however, the Church, led by the Spirit, likewise continued to grow into a fuller understanding of its identity, structural make-up, and mission. As I will show later in this paper, when the Church opened its doors to biblical research and sought to examine the foundations of faith, renewed studies in christology started to bring about change both in ecclesiology and anthropology. Similarly, changes in society and in the Church provided new optics through which to deepen the meaning of the mystery of Christ.

II. VATICAN II

A. Anthropology

During this period, the people of the periphery—that is, the marginated, oppressed, and rejected of the world, such as blacks and colonized peoples—started to reject their unequal status. Likewise, some of the people in developed nations began to accept partial responsibility for the racist and classist divisions of the world. They formulated plans to assist the "underdeveloped" peoples to come out of their misery. At the basis of their proposals was the assumption that these people were not born inferior, but had just not developed properly. Hence, theirs was not a natural inferiority but simply a cultural one; underdeveloped cultures had, therefore, to be helped to come up to the developed cultures of the world, that is, to the standards of civilization. Because the Western, developed nations viewed themselves as the normative model of what it meant to be human, they were eager to help "less developed" people. This happened not only on the global level, but also on the national; in the United States, for instance, plans were established to "bring up" minorities to the norms of the developed cultures.

Such attempts were admirable; but often the effects were disastrous, because at the core of the development model, "progress" was defined according to the norms of the white, European-North American bourgeois. Development meant dying to one's own heritage, so as to arise a white Westerner. At the root of this model, moreover, lay the conviction that the world's problems would be solved when the underdeveloped became like the white Western nations. Development would bring utopia.

The naiveté of this vision is now so obvious. Yes, Western civilization had indeed contributed much to the advancement of humanity, but it likewise had contributed much to its destruction: the atomic bomb, two world wars, secularization, nihilism, materialism, atheism, the myth of upward mobility, alcoholism, drug addiction, and the breakdown of family life. Scientific and technological advances enabled average citizens of the West to be very comfortable, but bereft of meaning in their lives.

Yet in the years preceding Vatican II, the West was virtually blind to its defects. Seeing only its achievements and advantages, scores of programs and millions of people went out with immense goodwill to help in the development of peoples. These were the new religious: the humanitarian, technological, and educational missionaries. Now the priest-missioner was regarded as an expert who had something of human value to offer the underdeveloped peoples of the world; the professionals became new high priests who could provide everyone with solutions. They could often diagnose people's problems, even without asking them.

In sum, while the world now recognized its inequality, it was convinced that the unity of humankind would be brought about by helping the so-called underdeveloped, inferior people of the world become like Westerners. Technology could do this rapidly, and human perfection appeared to be within reach.

B. Ecclesiology

The Council Fathers of Vatican II rather immediately saw the elaboration of a meaningful ecclesiology as one of their most pressing tasks. This meant not new dogmatic formulas, but a relevant, pastoral presentation of the Church's self-identity and mission. Among all the documents of Vatican II, the Constitution on the Church (**Lumen Gentium**) was the most passionately debated and drastically revised document. Its understanding and interpretation of the nature and mission of the Church were, in my opinion, more powerful than any new dogmatic statement could have been. The theological depth of the constitution meant that, while the tradition of the Church was affirmed, it also engendered a new emphasis: the Church at the service of humanity.

From a serious study of fonts of revelation, Vatican II proclaimed: "Before all things, however, the kingdom is clearly visible in the very person of Christ, the Son of God and Son of Man, who came 'to **serve** and to give His life as ransom for many' (Mark 10:45)" (LG #5). The Council went on to proclaim that it is "the **community** of faith, hope, and charity" (LG #8). These people of God are "a living **witness** to Him, especially by means of a life of faith and charity and by offering to God a sacrifice of praise, the tribute of lips which give honor to His name (cf. Heb. 13:15)" (LG #12; emphasis added). In these texts, we find the three key words of the model of the Church of Vatican II: **witness** (to teach), **service** (to rule), and **community fellowship** (to sanctify). They are a very biblical way of expressing the threefold mission of all Christians.

It became obvious that, in order to be a servant church in the midst of the world, ordination or profession of vows would not alone suffice. Accordingly, priests and religious enrolled in universities to specialize in counseling, communications, religious education, hospital work, social work, and other human services. Thus began the age of professional church workers which is probably best marked by the appearance of professionally prepared lay theologians, M.A.'s in religious education and M.Div.'s in seminary education. Universities, however, often did not accept seminary-earned credits, and professional certification became the prime qualification for church work. University programs for professional preparation of ministers proliferated, and seminaries evolved into professional schools of divinity.

As more human needs were identified, more professionals were in demand. Though the church was spoken of as a community, it functioned as a new bureaucracy; like the government's, its budget for the necessary professionals skyrocketed. Ironically, one seemingly had to be a millionaire to be able to serve the poor and to respond to unending needs of the world.

The new high priests of the church of Vatican II were no longer the ordained hierarchy, but the academicians and experts. They drew the crowds, wrote the books, and influenced the thinking of those preparing to serve. No longer now did only the ecclesiastically appointed authorities control knowledge and rites. A new hierarchy emerged which was based not on appointment from on high, but rather on the merits of a recognized expertise. The people listened to those whose erudition offered insight and wisdom. In practice, infallibility was more easily accorded to certain key thinkers—theologians or biblical scholars—than to the official magisterium. The Church had, in effect, passed from an episcopal hierarchy to an academic-professional one.

But for the masses of the people at the bottom of the pyramid, nothing had really changed. Now they were spoken to (one might even say dictated to) by two authorities: the episcopal **and** the academic. Whom were they to believe? Under the leadership of these authorities, many studies were done to ascertain the peoples' needs to determine what programs would best answer those needs. But the resultant plans and programs were always those of the experts; ministry was viewed as doing things for people in a professional way, and usually at professional wages. But the people themselves were seldom consulted or listened to; they still were simply told what to do and were expected to accept immediately and without question the decisions of the new authority.

The servant-model of ministry and preparation was a great advance in the understanding of Christian ministry. Nonetheless, one significant distortion of the meaning of ministry characterized the age. The Church, not unlike other enslaved peoples in the early stages of their liberation, looked to others for models of development. In looking outside itself, the Church was trying to be like the world.

Thus the only normative image the Church had of "service" was that of the world. And, conversely, the only normative model of "apostolate" the world had was that of the clergy. So, full-time Church workers wanting to serve the world had to become professionals. On the other hand, laity who were called to exercise the universal priesthood of Christians had only one model of priesthood: the clergy in the sanctuary. This "development stage" has led to the deep identity crisis of the present Church.[6] The clergy and religious wanted to get into the world in order to serve, and the laity wanted to get into the sanctuary in order to be apostolic. Professional preparation was required for ordination, but ordination was not required for professional preparation. New questions of identity arose. Is the full-time ministerial service of religious and clergy any different from other well-intentioned public services? Where, if anywhere, is priestly or religious originality? Wherein is the difference between Christian ministry and other service-oriented jobs? What is the originality or uniqueness of Christian ministry?

So, by seeking to serve the world well, the Church had converted to the ways of the world, and, consequently, was blinded by the very structures it was supposed to redeem. The service models of the world have now become normative for the models of the Church, and the ministerial models of the clergy have become normative for laity who want to share in the apostolate. Furthermore, professional salaries for the increasing number of ministerial professionals continue to increase much faster than either the rate of inflation or the price of gasoline. Will the Church ever be able to respond to all the needs? Will it replace government agencies and private means of serving others? Wherein is the uniqueness of the "service" which the Church is to render in the world?

C. Christology

Even though there is no explicit christology in the documents of Vatican II, an implicit one runs through them, and especially through **Lumen Gentium.** In this document, and in the general thinking of the Church since its promulgation, the predominant christological emphasis has been that of the humanity of Christ, **The Son of Man,** healing, forgiving, praying, reconciling, welcoming, befriending, and feasting. The principal image has been that of the good shepherd who comes to serve and not to be served. This certainly images beautifully the ministry of our Lord. But as the overemphasis on divinity tended to diminish the human aspect, so this stress on the human aspect alone has tended to diminish appreciation of the totality and integrity of the Christ-event.

Without doubt, attention to the humanity of Jesus has brought the Lord much closer to people's personal lives. But this focus can degenerate too easily into a portrayal of Jesus as a sort of a "super Mr. Nice Guy." Despite the appeal of such an image, it may mask or hide the most profound aspects of the life and message of Jesus the Christ. The danger is in its legitimizing a superficial nicety rather than calling Christians to a total conversion of the heart. Ultimately only this **metanoia** can truly liberate persons and peoples from the multiple enslavements of the established structures of the world.

III. JOHN PAUL II AND PUEBLA

A. Anthropology

From the early 1960s, the whole developmental schema began to be questioned radically by the natives of the Third World countries and by blacks, Hispanics, and Native Americans of the United States; more recently, some of the non-Anglo-Saxon European immigrants have added their own questions.

As the peoples who had been labelled "underdeveloped" by the rich and powerful rejected this nomenclature, they likewise affirmed their own identity and uniqueness. The blacks in the United States proclaimed, "Black is beautiful," and other minority groups similarly spoke proudly of their own heritages. The peoples who had been made to think of themselves as inferior no longer wanted to imitate what had previously been regarded as normative models. Moreover, they even pointed out many of the defects of the heretofore unquestioned model; the so-called "developed peoples" were actually "underdeveloped" in many aspects of life. Thus they could not serve as a model for anyone. Pluralism was encouraged; it became evident that diverse cultural models of society, each with its own proper institutions, logic, knowledge, language, and religious symbols, were necessary for the humanization of the world.

People now began to recognize that universities had monopolized and dominated knowledge for the benefit of those who financed the institutions and to the detriment of those who were exploited by the benefactors. The realization was dawning that the dominant group, who created knowledge for its own well-being and survival, maintained an absolute monopoly on certifying the educated person. The very peoples whom the universities labelled as "problems" of society recognized instead that it was the financial schemes of the rich which victimized society.[7] Not only was Western knowledge being questioned, but also the sacrosanct institutions which were proclaiming it.

Vietnam, civil rights movements, Wounded Knee, Watts, the riots at the National Democratic Convention in Chicago, Kent State, Martin Luther King, Jr., Cesar Chavez: a new era was beginning! The legitimacy and purity of the American (U.S.A.) way—meaning "WASP"—was being radically questioned and challenged. People now recognized that they could be American without accepting the WASP model. "American (U.S.A.), YES! WASP, NO! We are not a melting-pot, but a stew-pot."

What was happening in the United States was happening around the world. Peoples of the Third World wanted to better the human condition, but they did not want simply to trade their ways for those of the North Atlantic cultural groups. The formerly colonized peoples rejected every type of colonization: political-economic, intellectual, religious, and cultural.

Education itself, long thought to be a neutral service, was suddenly challenged at its very roots by such prophetic giants as Paulo Freire in his classic **Pedagogy of the Oppressed**, and Ivan Illich in his **De-schooling Society.** It was recognized that education had not liberated people, but had enslaved them by turning them into robots of Western civilization.

The new anthropology affirms the basic equality of all persons and holds that the authentic unity of the human race can only come through a respect for differences. Thus people ought not to try to become like everyone else, but rather to develop themselves in their own way to the fullness of their being. In this anthropology, unity lies not in uniformity but in difference.

In describing this momentum among various ethnic and radical groups, I do not want to imply that these ideas are generally accepted. In fact, judging from the growing racist manifestations in the U.S.A., I would dare to say that a good portion of the dominant white population of the North Atlantic is still in the mentality first described in this paper. For the most part, the white, Western world still considers itself biologically and culturally superior to all others. The churches and the universities want to do things for minorities, but are very threatened when the minorities want to set up their own institutions. Well-intentioned liberals of the North Atlantic cultures are very comfortable with the "developmental" model, but defensive and insecure with a liberation model allowing for diverse ways of thinking, reasoning, and doing. It is most difficult for missionaries sent from the First World to accept the fact that they are not superior to the people to whom they are sent, but merely different; they need to see themselves not merely as teachers, but also as learners. The greatest challenge to modern-day missioners is to be agents of the gospel of our Lord Jesus Christ, not agents of the gospel of their own cultural identity with a thin veneer of Christian terminology and ideas.

Within this emergent anthropology is an awareness that people cannot simply be told or dictated to, but must be listened to. People must be taken seriously in a way which respects their human dignity; each person has something of value to say and to offer. Precisely because one sees oneself as someone of worth, one sets out to develop one's potential to the fullest.

Among the deepest forms of oppression of the world's poor has been that the rich, the powerful, and the educated have convinced the oppressed that they are not good for anything, that they are inferior human beings, and that they have, in effect, nothing to offer but their cheap labor and weak bodies. The normative image which the North Atlantic cultures have managed to propagate of themselves is one of the deepest forms of contemporary enslavement.

The great irony today is that people in the North Atlantic world are reviving the philosophy of nihilism, asking, "Why live?" Meanwhile, the oppressed and poor of the world, whose life-expectancy is far below that of their First World brothers and sisters, are still asking themselves the question, "Why do we have to die so far ahead of our time?"

B. Ecclesiology

Pope John XXIII expressed some marvelous intuitions which were left undeveloped by Vatican II. Even though it was the first Council to have a significant representation of non-European voices, the church of the North Atlantic nations dominated. Hence, the extreme and multi-faceted poverty of the rest of the world did not become a major issue at Vatican II, though **Lumen Gentium** #8 does deal with it in part, and some mention was made in other sections. The proposed Schema XIV, an explicit discussion of poverty, never was completed.

Nevertheless, Pope Paul VI, the great champion of the dignity, rights, and mission of the poor, far surpassed Vatican II in **Populorum Progressio, Octogesima Adveniens, Evangelii Nuntiandi,** and his address to the United Nations. His line of thought in relation to the mission and struggles of the poor has been picked up and given greater emphasis by Pope John Paul II.[8]

While the churches of the North Atlantic sought to renew liturgical celebration, religious education programs, and ministries of service to the people of God, the churches of the Third World[9] struggled to join their people in moving from a miserable existence into a more human way of life. Indeed, the leaders of these peoples rapidly realized that their misery was not just an accident of nature and of history; it resulted from the strategy of the world's powerful, who had to keep the poor enslaved so as to insure the well-being of the rich. Thus, the powerful had no self-interest in change. The poor themselves had to lead the process of transformation.

Sadly, most citizens of the First World have no idea that their generally prosperous standard of living results not entirely from their own hard work and dedication, but rather from exploitation of the poor and from rape of their natural resources. The West has been able to develop its comfortable level of existence and its concomitant feeling of superiority by causing the poor to become poorer and, ultimately, to lose their sense of self-worth. Thus the matter of poverty is structural rather than personal: the structures of the world allow the rich to become richer and, consequently, to rob the middle class and poor.

But some Christians who recognized this structural evil have begun to reread the Gospel in a very serious way and to reexamine various aspects of ecclesiology. If the Gospel is indeed the Good News, then what might this Good News mean in the poor regions of the world? Even more, what is the transforming power of the Gospel in the rich countries of the world?[10]

The Church of Vatican II may be characterized as the witnessing community of service; in practice that meant that those who had more education and resources (according to the standards of the world) as well as a certain amount of good will and dedication, were sent to help the less fortunate. The Church of John Paul II and Puebla, however, inverts the formula: those who have less will initiate the liberation and salvation of the more fortunate ones of the world. It is the Church of the poor which now invites all others to join them in their new life of the Spirit. This in itself is the sign that the Kingdom has begun!

It is those who have less, the **materially poor,**[11] who are the "**predilectos de Dios,**" the "favored ones of God." They have the greatest potential of becoming Church and of carrying the Gospel to the rest of the world, because, at the very core of the Good News is the fact that those who seemingly have nothing to offer have in fact the greatest gift to offer the whole world. The preferential, though not exclusive, regard for the poor is the most characteristic word of John Paul II and Puebla.

Pope Paul VI, John Paul II, and Puebla have announced to everyone that the materially poor have a special place and a special mission in God's salvific plan for the world. In speaking on evangelization as the essential mission of the Church, Paul VI stated on December 8, 1975:

> As the kernel and center of His Good News, Christ proclaims salvation, this great gift of God which is liberation from everything that oppresses man. . . . (EN #9)

> Christ accomplished this proclamation of the Kingdom of God through the untiring preaching of a word. . . . (EN #11)

> But Christ also carried out this proclamation by innumerable signs, which amazed the crowds and at the same time drew them to Him in order to see Him, listen to Him, and allow themselves to be transformed by Him: . . . **at the center of all this there is one to which He attaches**

great importance: the humble and the poor are evangelized, become His disciples, and gather together "in His name" in the great community of those who believe in Him . . . He had come and was to die "to gather together in unity the scattered children of God." (EN #12)

The very personal and preferential love of John Paul II for the afflicted, the suffering, the poor, and the silenced was evident in both the spontaneous actions and formal presentations of his journey to Mexico. In speaking about the essential characteristic of the Christian ministry of liberation, the Pope gave the following as a criterion of authenticity:

> In what form they lovingly care for the poor, the sick, the dispossessed, the neglected, and the oppressed and in what way they find in them the image of the poor and suffering Jesus, and strive to relieve their need and serve Christ in them. (LG #8, as quoted in "Pope to Bishops of Puebla," III.6)

January 29, 1979, the Pope went on to tell the Indian peasants of Cuilapan:

> The Pope wants to be your voice, the voice of those who cannot speak or who are silenced, to be the conscience of consciences, the invitation to action, in order to make up for lost time, a time that is frequently one of prolonged suffering and of unfulfilled hopes.

> With him [Pope Paul VI], I want to repeat—and if it is possible, in an even stronger voice—that the current Pope wants to be "linked to your cause, the cause of the poor countries, of the poor people," (speech to Farmworkers, Pope Paul VI, Colombia, August 23, 1978); that the Pope is with this mass of population, "almost always abandoned to an ignoble level of life and at times treated and exploited harshly."

The Supreme Pontiff desires to affirm, to teach, and to proclaim the truths of the concrete struggles for justice of the people who are repressed and silenced by society.

What previous popes have pointed to, the bishops of Puebla stated directly, clearly, and without reservation. They say: **"El compromiso preferencial con los pobres y oprimidos y el incremento de las Comunidades de Base"**; the commitment of the Church to the poor has helped to discover **"el potencial evangelizador de los pobres"** insofar as the poor constantly question society, inviting it to conversion (Puebla #911). The poor are the **"primeros destinatarios"** of the mission of Jesus, and their

evangelization is the supreme sign that the kingdom has begun
(#906, citing Luke 18-21; 7:21-23).[12]

Thus the starting point of Christian mission is the materially
poor. The Gospel begins among the victims of injustice, the hungry, the ugly, the sick, the dying, the handicapped, the marginated,
the rejected, the excluded of society. In and through such peoples
does the God of Jesus make himself seen and known. God initiated
salvation through the poor of Israel; in fidelity to God's way, the
Church must continually begin with the poor. Among the poor who
hear the Word and are converted, the Church becomes the dynamic
community of joy and hope based on a living faith, prayer, and
love. In solidarity with **their** struggle only, will the prosperous, the
accepted, the dignified, the beautiful, the educated, the professional, the religious find salvation. The poor carry salvation to the
rest of the world! They call everyone to conversion to God through
them. In the poor God is revealed.

In the reception of the Spirit through baptism, human curse is
converted into blessing. The very suffering of the people—their
rejection, their dispossession, their powerlessness, their condem-
nation to silence—is transformed into a dynamic energy which will
initiate new forms of human existence so that others will not have
to suffer what they have had to suffer. The greater the suffering has
been, the greater will be the potential for evangelization.[13] The
poor are not asked to resign themselves to their misery, but, in the
power of the Spirit, to initiate new life which will break through
and transcend the rich-poor dialectic of the world.

The poor alone cannot change the way things are, because they
do not possess the knowledge and technology necessary for
changing society. But neither can the scientist, the professional,
nor the religious leader alone bring about a liberating transformation. The two need each other; the poor provide the creative and
liberating spirit, and the others offer the know-how and techniques.
Without this spirit, know-how and technology will simply confirm
the status quo. Without the critical questioning of the marginal
peoples, society will merely continue to improve for those who are
comfortable. A profoundly innovative transformation can only be
initiated by the outsider, or by those who renounce power and
prestige.[14] Renunciation of the powers of this world enables one to
be filled with the power of the transforming and creative spirit. Has
this not been the example of Jesus, of St. Francis Assisi and of

Mother Teresa of Calcutta? This free renunciation of wealth for the sake of solidarity with the poor can truly be called evangelical poverty.[15]

Today the Church needs both ordained ministers of religion and well-qualified professionals. But beyond the fundamental call and preparation, Christians in ministry need to be in solidarity with the poor of the world. To minister as Christians they must enter into the lives of the poor, listen with great love, respect and patience, and assume their misery and their struggles. The most essential part of Christian formation is not the intellectual learning, but the living, daily communion and participation in the life of the materially poor of the world. The educated, both ordained and professional, who are Christian ministers, must enter into solidarity with the poor of the world. Together with them, and from within their structures, a salvific, liberating team might develop for the transformation of all society.[16]

Today the final verification of the authenticity and legitimacy of the Christian minister is neither ordination nor degree, but the holiness and fidelity of lifestyle:

> For the Church, the first means of evangelization is the witness of an authentically Christian life, given over to God in a communion that nothing should destroy it and at the same time to one's neighbor with limitless zeal.
>
> Modern man listens more willingly to witnesses than to teachers, and if he does not listen to teachers, it is because they are not witnesses . . . .
>
> It is therefore, primarily by Her conduct and by Her life that the Church will evangelize the world, in other words by Her living witness of fidelity to the Lord Jesus—**the witness of poverty and detachment, of freedom in the face of the powers of this world,** in short, a witness of sanctity. (EN #41; emphasis added).[17]

Ordained priests and bishops, as well as professional people, are needed to function in the world while giving witness that they are not of the world. The power of Christian ministry has its source not in worldly powers, but in the mystery of the cross and resurrection. Ultimately the legitimacy of ministry is found in the poverty which ministers accept for the sake of the Kingdom and for the sake of solidarity with the poor, among whom the Kingdom is already beginning.

Let nothing obscure this reality; the Christian minister is called to follow the Lord, leaving all things and following his way rather than one's own. The more authority one has in the Church— hierarchical, religious, professional, academic—the more one has voluntarily to renounce the riches and prestige of this world so as to live among the poor in their manner of life. Simplicity of life is indeed a Christian ideal in itself, for it indicates a liberation from the idols of materialism. In contrast, material poverty and destitution are not ideals by any standard whatsoever, but the direct result of the sinful greed of the rich. Thus one chooses to live in poverty among the victims of injustice, not because it is an ideal existence, but precisely because it is a way of taking on oneself the sin of the world. Jesus, who was totally without sin, took onto himself the sinful human condition in order that he might liberate all from sin (2 Cor. 5:21). So too with the followers of Christ; they freely take on the condition brought about by sin—material poverty in all its forms—in order to liberate everyone.

The higher one rises in the hierarchy of church ministry, the more one's life must conform to that of the Supreme Authority, Jesus. Freely chosen poverty and freely accepted suffering for the sake of others are the most vivid signs of the personal holiness and fidelity of the minister of Christ.

Highly paid professionals in the Church might competently render some very necessary services, but they are not thereby giving Christian witness. Simply because one works for the Church, one is not necessarily a Christian minister. Ministry is not to be equated with rendering valuable professional services and being the recipient of a professional wage. A lifestyle of poverty should be freely chosen by the person and not imposed by the employer— even when the employer is the church. In the past, it has not been uncommon to confuse a chosen lifestyle of poverty with unjust, low wages.

At the root of Christian ministry is witness, the new lifestyle based on conversion from the way of the world to the way of the Lord. For those involved in Christian education, degrees, ordination, titles, and publications cannot be the final qualification for teaching. The first and indispensable qualification for a Christian teacher is a personal lifestyle of freely chosen material poverty in solidarity with the poor, who alone can teach the world the full measure of the continual suffering brought about by sin. Only when the world fully appreciates this suffering will it yearn for salvation. Like Jesus, his followers must assume the sinful condition (poverty) without sinning (wealth). This is the **condition sine qua non** of the Christian educator[18] and minister.

The formation of future ministers, whether ordained, professional, or lay must include the development of attitudes of profound love for and solidarity with the poor of the world, coupled with a burning zeal for the elimination of poverty itself. This love of the poor but hatred of poverty, like love of the criminal but hatred of crime, cannot be an abstraction or classroom lesson alone. It will only come about through Scripture reading, prayer, meditation, self-denial, discipline, and arduous study; above all, it will result from actually living and working among the poorest of society.

Without this base, the best of university and seminary studies will be sterile, artificial, and empty. On the other hand, mere solidarity with the poor without serious intellectual and spiritual formation will have nothing of value to offer the poor, except mediocre service. There is no substitute for knowledge and genuine Christian spirituality. To be with and serve the poor in a simplistic way can easily become a mockery of the poor that is in actuality a romantic response to the need to be needed by others. The poor cannot be used to provide a feeling of fulfillment.

Formation, therefore, must be serious and sufficiently long so as to digest and assimilate the necessary matter. The future minister needs to be in contact both with the best elements of the Christian tradition and with the sciences that provide the technical know-how to carry out the work. But ministerial preparation must always pose the questions and seek direction, not from the perspective of the established ways, but from the perspective of those who have been abused by them and excluded from participation. Studies are necessary; but, one must ask, from whose viewpoint and on whose behalf am I studying? Each person comes to education from a specific perspective and with specific goals, even if the deepest ones are usually subconscious. The questions in Christian education are these: Who ultimately am I with? Who am I for? What am I against? Educators cannot remain in abstract generalities, for to do so is to rob the Gospel of its greatest energy. They must particularize and put flesh and blood onto the abstractions, lest the generalities and universal ideas hide the real ugliness and pain of the suffering of the destitute of the world. One cannot only be for humanity; one must be **for** certain specific expressions of humanity and, consequently, clearly **against** others. To remain in the realm of universals is to lose awareness of the real sin of the world destroying not only individual persons, but entire peoples. To speak and think in generalities is to miss the transforming energy of the Gospel penetrating not only human hearts, but every stratum of human society.[19]

The only starting point for eradicating sin and bringing the Kingdom lies with the victims of the sin of the world. Solidarity with the poor proclaims the truth of God's universal love by denouncing sin in the historical and concrete mechanisms of the world and by announcing the kind of Kingdom to which **everyone** is invited. It is this supreme truth which the Christian minister must live and proclaim; it is an invitation to all, but especially to the rich and the powerful of the world, to repent and be converted. They are the ones in greatest need of total **metanoia;** their ways hurt not only them, but the rest of the people of the world.

Christians who do their task effectively will inevitably be persecuted. The rich and powerful do not want their own **metanoia,** but instead the resignation of the poor so that they will stay submissive, hardworking, "happy" people. Persecution and martyrdom, not popular programs and impressive statistics, are the authentic guarantees that Christian ministers are truly accomplishing their tasks.

The Christian minister, in the style of Jesus, does not seek to do things alone, but to call others to recognize their talents and abilities for the good of the community. The energy released by the minister in calling people forth to service is endless; such calling of others is the minister's main task. Everyone without exception has something of value to offer. The challenge of the minister is to help each person discover his or her own particular charisms and to utilize these gifts in a ministry for the common good.

As a community of ministers grows, each serving according to his or her capacity, the specific task of the ordained or full-time minister will be to animate the common struggle. It is not his or her task to do everything, nor primarily to administer the institution. Rather the principal task of the ordained minister is to enable people to do things for themselves and to be the center of their unity, thus animating by the power of personal example the word of God and the breaking of the bread. It is in the festive celebration of God's concrete actions in history on behalf of the weak and defenseless that God's liberating and unifying power will be experienced.

The need presently exists to avoid the dichotomy between ordained minister and professional; the solution lies not in eliminating one group or another, but by recognizing the validity of both. Their unity and complementarity will be discovered as both ordained and professionals enter into a living solidarity with the poorest of their world. The poor provide the necessary spirit to render an authentically Christian witness.

Not only is the word of God permanent, but also lasting is God's relationship with the world as it is. From the beginning, the God of Judaic and Christian traditions has been the God who has seen people's suffering, heard their cries, and acted to save them. The Christian message begins by listening to the concrete cries and sufferings of people. From within the situation of suffering and in solidarity with the cry for salvation, the Church must reread its fundamental constitution, the Gospel of our Lord Jesus Christ. Through such a rereading from the perspective of the poor, the fullness of the hidden and dynamic energy of the Gospel will shine forth. Thus, the final word the Church has to offer the world is not merely doctrines and teachings, but a living tradition, beginning with the preparation in Israel, coming into its fullness in Jesus, and continuing as the Church strives to respond to the real sufferings and enslavements of society. This message will truly be good news to the poor and a word of judgment to those responsible for the situation of misery.[20]

C. Christology

If at one point the Church emphasized the divinity of Christ and then at another his humanity, today it is beginning to turn its attention to the divine Christ of eternal power.[21] He did not consider equality with God something to be held onto, but "he emptied himself and took the form of a slave, being born in the likeness of men. He was known to be of human estate and it was thus he humbled himself, obediently accepting even death, death on the cross" (Phil. 2:6-8). Jesus became an absolute nobody, even a scandal. Yet in this lonely and despised man, the Father revealed himself and invites people to himself.

In this abasement or self-effacement of Christ is the model for authentic Christian service. He who had all the dignity in the world did not hesitate to divest himself of his divine prerogative, but emptied himself in order to become one among the enslaved and the poor of the world.[22]

Today it is possible to penetrate the multiple layers of theological reflection of the evangelists and the early Christian Church in order to get a good glimpse of the reality of the historical Jesus of Nazareth.[23] Only in the total mystery of Christ—from the very beginning to the very end[24]—will Christians know how Jesus, the Son of God, truly functioned and related to both persons and the structures of his society. The way of the historical Jesus of Nazareth alone is normative for anyone wanting to be his disciple. There is no other way.

The questions today focus not so much on "Who really was Jesus of Nazareth?" In faith one has no doubt that he was true God of true God, and true man of true man. But now, these are the significant questions: "How did this Jesus live and function in this world?" "What was his wordly identity?" "How did he relate to others?" The relationship between Jesus and the people and structures of his society is **constitutive** of the way the followers of Christ today must relate to similar peoples and structures in present society. Time and space change but the human condition remains fundamentally the same. The image, the cultural identity, and the relationships of Jesus are all essential elements of the Good News, then, today, and always.

Thus, it is important to see in the **kenosis** of Jesus the model for all Christian ministers. He who had all the power and the glory did not hesitate to empty himself of it in order to come into the world in full solidarity with the poor, the marginated, the unprestigious, the unlettered, the lay people. (Jesus was not a priest according to the religion of his day.) It was from within this identity that Jesus initiated a new way which he in turn offers to everyone. Today God likewise continues to invite all to salvation through the way of Jesus. Jesus is in solidarity with the poor; he, however, is not just another poor, illiterate person, but one who speaks with great liberty and authority. He scandalizes all with his wisdom, because he was the carpenter from Galilee, the son of Mary.

Jesus was willing to accept death in order to remain totally obedient to the Father's will and thereby to save humanity by the power of unlimited love. But if from the divine perspective the crucifixion can be seen as the act of redemption, from the human point of view it must be recognized in its historical sense as the assassination of a man who had disturbed the system by rejecting its hypocrisy and exploitation. Because Jesus was a deeply religious man, he was condemned by the establishment of his world and accused of being a political subversive.

Precisely in this total self-giving is Jesus exalted to the highest dignity by the Father. "Because of this, God highly exalted him and bestowed on him the name above every other name, so that at Jesus' name every knee must bend in the heavens, on the earth, and under the earth, and every tongue proclaim to the glory of God the Father, Jesus Christ is Lord" (Phil. 2:9-11).

Only a deep appreciation for the significance of Jesus' **kenosis** will overcome the dichotomies of the divine and human natures of Christ. Furthermore, this model of the incarnation continues to serve as a pattern for every Christian minister.

There are certainly many noble and praiseworthy ways of rendering human service without having to enter into total solidarity with others. Only one way, however, of Christian ministry exists, from which no one—pope, bishops, priests, religious professionals, or laity—is excused: discipleship in the concrete and specific way of Jesus. The more authority that one receives from the Church, the greater the obligation one has to follow the footsteps of the Lord. This is the only authentic way of exercising authority; this is the only type of authority that will astonish others and lead them to follow the Lord. The more that authority, whether hierarchical or academic, is faithful to the way of Jesus, the more it will be a true service:

> All "sacred power" exercised in the Church is nothing other than service, service with a single purpose: to insure that all the people of God share in this three-fold mission of Christ and always remain under the power of the Lord, power that has its source not in the powers of this world but in the mystery of the cross and resurrection.[25]

Ministry and Education from a Pastoral-Theological Perspective

FIELD OF STUDY	PRE-VATICAN II TIMES	TIMES OF VATICAN II	TIMES OF JOHN PAUL II AND PUEBLA
Anthropology	**Inequality** Racist-classist society prevails White Western man... (normative model for all)	**Equality in Sameness** People can become equal... (to us, the normative group)	**Equality in Difference** People are equal in their differences...(no universal normative model)
Ecclesiology	**The Sacral-Hierarchical Society...the institute**	**The Witnessing Community of Service...the community**	**A Charismatic-Liberating Group...the leaven**
a. **ministry**	Ordained or consecrated	The professional	The baptized
b. **preparation**	Seminary or novitiate	University or professional school	Solidarity with dispossessed and suffering
c. **verification**	Ordination or vows	Degree or certificate	Holiness and fidelity: life of evangelical poverty
d. **authority**	Domination	Service	Truth: teachers of love and builders of unity
e. **main task**	Teach, rule, and sanctify	Witness, service, fellowship	Martyrdom, calling forth ministers, animating the common struggle
f. **"Last word"**	Pope and bishops	The experts	The word of God in the light of the concrete needs of the people
Christology	**Son of God** (emphasis on divinity)	**Son of Man** (emphasis on humanity)	**Kenosis:** The humiliation-exaltation of Christ (emphasis on the full human meaning and function of the Incarnation: transcendent love of God visible in the weakness of Jesus)

Summary of Paper presented at Boston College on November 10, 1979, by Virgil P. Elizondo

NOTES

1. I write as a pastoral theologian. Hence, I am not entering here into dogmatic and ontological notions of priesthood, church, and ministry, but simply into the way these terms appear to function in today's society. I will be happy to leave to others the scriptural and dogmatic questions involved here. My paper will be more descriptive of the way these realities appear to function in the Church's ongoing growth, development, and self-understanding of its identity and mission.

2. In speaking about these realities I do not want to imply that all the people have these concepts and agree with them. It is rather the visionaries and the avant-garde who begin to see reality in the way that I will explain it under the three categories mentioned.

3. I purposely use the term "man" because at this time neither women nor women's views were considered of any great value.

4. See Avery Dulles' commentary on **Lumen Gentium** in the Abbot translation of the documents of Vatican II.

5. It is interesting how, for the masses of the people of Spain and Latin America who have traditionally been outside any and every established power structure, it has always been the figure of the Nazarene (the suffering Jesus) which has fascinated the people. Even the image of Christ the King assumed a totally different meaning in Mexico, where it became the standard bearer for the **Cristero** revolution. Whereas in Europe, the figure of Christ the King seemed to legitimize and strengthen the status quo, in Latin America it became the symbol that no human establishment could be trusted and that trust could be placed only in Christ, the King. Hence in Europe it functioned as a reactionary image, while in Latin America, it has functioned as a revolutionary image. For those in power, "Christ" is the more important title; for the poor and marginated, it is "Jesus" which is the more significant.

6. For a more detailed explanation of the characteristics of the development stage and of the subsequent liberation stage, consult this author's **Christianity and Culture** (Huntington, Ind.: Our Sunday Visitor Press, 1975), pp. 140-148.

7. For some very interesting and illuminating discussions, consult W. Ryan's **Blaming the Victim** (New York: Image Books, 1972).

8. Consult his addresses in Mexico, in particular his address to the bishops, his address to the people of Cuilapan, his address to the people at Zapopan, and his address to the workers at Monterrey.

9. **Third World.** In this section I use the term, not only in reference to the Third World countries, but to all the peoples who are "materially poor," as defined in n. #11.

10. I have frequently heard it said that it is dangerous and discomforting for the powerful and the rich to read the gospels. And as I reread

them with my people and the suffering peoples of the world, I can see more and more the reason for this statement. It is no surprise to me that the **Magnificat** has been prohibited in Argentina today. Furthermore, I have heard it said, and agree from my observations, that the established and powerful seek to know Christ while the poor and oppressed seek to know the historical Jesus of Nazareth.

11. I use the term **materially poor** so as to be very clear. I am not speaking of the so-called "spiritually poor," but of what the popes describe as the dispossessed, the marginated, the victims of unjust wages, the physically hungry and starving, those malformed by malnutrition and disease, and the filthy, who have no sanitary conditions. The term refers to those who have neither material goods, nor voice, nor human dignity. Their living conditions are a scandal and a contradiction to Christian existence. The "spiritually poor" are those who have freely chosen solidarity with the poor with all the consequence this implies—one with their life, sufferings, dreams, and struggles.

12. For a good discussion of the exact and unequivocal meaning of "poor" in all these texts, I refer the reader to the concrete descriptions of "poor" in the speeches of John Paul II in Mexico and to Gustavo Gutierrez' "Pobres y Liberacion en Puebla," April, 1979, pp. 21-22.

13. For a much fuller development of this point consult this author's work, **Mestizaje—the Dialectic of Cultural Birth and the Gospel** (San Antonio: Mexican American Cultural Center, 1978).

14. Refer to Pope John Paul's talk to the Indians at Cuilapan, January 29, 1979.

15. There is nothing that could in any sense of the word be called "Good News" when one sees the concrete reality of poverty: rat-infested neighborhoods, lacking running water or electricity, with numerous children dying because of disease and malnutrition, people dying of simple diseases because of lack of medicine, and people with nothing to do because of lack of employment.

What could ever be evangelical about poverty? Evangelical poverty means not the idealization of poverty, but the free acceptance of life among the poor for the sake of solidarity with the victims of the injustice of the world. Solidarity with them in life and in word is a living protest to the lifestyle of a sinful society, which can live in comfort and luxury at the expense of the misery of others. Furthermore, such a solidarity with the poor in their struggles aims to bring about bold, creative, and rapid transformation; it is "evangelical" because their struggle should lead to new lifestyles for everyone that will do away with the sin of the world which perpetuates the sinful relationship of the rich and poor.

It is called "evangelical poverty"—the good news of poverty—because out of the refusal to resign oneself to the dehumanizing misery, and out of the refusal to develop oneself in imitation of the ways of those who have brought about and perpetuate this misery, one dares to risk in the spirit a radically new style of life.

16. Pope's talk to the Indians at Cuilapan, January 29, 1979.

17. On the same point, consult also #76 of **Evangelii Nuntiandi;** #23 and #45 of **Octogesimo;** speeches of John Paul II in Mexico and his various

exhortations to priests; and the presidential address of Archbishop John Quinn, the National Conference of Catholic Bishops, May 1, 1979: "The first service of the Church to the world is holiness and fidelity," in **Origins,** May 10, 1979.

18. For the role of the poor as the teachers of the world, consult Pope John Paul II's discourse to the Latin American Bishops III.6; also the speech delivered by Fr. Pedro Arrupe in San Antonio, Texas, on November 17, 1978, in which he stressed that the Jesuits, who are renowned throughout the world as educators, must now offer a new style of education to the world: their ability to learn from those who apparently have nothing to offer.

19. Consult **Evangelii Nuntiandi** #18, #19, and #20. Also **Redemptor Hominis,** #8 and #9; particularly on this point of not staying with the universal but going to the concrete and historical, consult #2, #16.

20. Consult John Paul II, talk to the Bishops in Puebla, Introduction; also, the very first speech delivered by Pope John Paul II on October 17, 1978.

21. For some good christologies which develop the full meaning of the **kenosis,** consult:
Henri Bourgeois, **Liberer Jesus,** (Paris: Le Centurion, 1977).
Jon Sobrino, **Christology at the Crossroads,** (New York: Orbis, 1978).
Jose Ignacio Gonzales-Faus, **La Humanidad Nueva,** (Madrid: EAPSA, 1975).
Jose Ignacio Gonzales-Faus, **Acceso A Jesus,** (Madrid: Sigueme, 1979).
Leonardo Boff, **Christ, Liberator of the Poor,** (New York: Orbis, 1978).
Christian DuQuoc, **Jesus, Hombre Libre,** (Madrid: Sigueme, 1975).
G. Theissen, **Le Christianisme De Jesus,** (Paris: Desclee, 1978).

22. For a fuller development of the full concrete meaning in sociocultural categories of the abasement of Christ, consult this author's **Mestizaje,** pp. 427-512.

23. R. Latourelle, **Finding Jesus Through the Gospels,** (New York: Alba House, 1979).

24. **Evangelii Nuntiandi** #12.

25. Inaugural homily of Pope John Paul II, October 22, 1978, in **Origins,** November 2, 1978.

QUESTIONS FOR DISCUSSION

1) Elizondo's typology is key to his paper, since he contends that ministry and education in the Church will be determined by the interplay among anthropology, ecclesiology, and christology. Do you agree with his description of each in the three periods delineated (pre-Vatican II, Vatican II, and John Paul II/Puebla), or would other data cause you to modify his categories in any respect?

2) What examples from your own life experience illumine or change Elizondo's description of the basic understandings in each of the three periods? What theological implications do you see in the order of his typology, in which ecclesiology precedes christology?

3) How do you see the materially poor having, as Elizondo writes, a "special place and a special mission in God's salvific plan for the world"?

4) Elizondo argues that the "most essential part of Christian formation is not the intellectual learning, but the living, daily communion and participation in the life of the materially poor of the world." He also maintains that "mere solidarity with the poor without serious intellectual and spiritual formation will have nothing of value to offer the poor, except mediocre service." What sort of formation for ministry would be able to encompass these points? How would you set up such a formation program?

5) How would you answer Elizondo's threefold question to educators: "Who ultimately am I with?" "Who am I for?" "What am I against?" What other questions might you pose as fundamental for religious education?

6) What impact has the increased employment of professionals had on the budget of ecclesiastical institutions with which you are familiar? Do you see professionalism as a healthy develop-

ment or as a situation creating a further rift between "specialists" and "laity" (i.e., nonspecialists)?

7) Can only those ministers who serve the Church in freely chosen poverty actually be considered "ministers"? Does the acceptance of a professional wage automatically eliminate one from consideration as a Christian minister? What, in your mind, would it mean to function in "freely chosen poverty"? Is Elizondo's argument here compatible with Schneiders' call for economic justice and professional integrity for ministers?

8) Elizondo intends to shift the focus from a preoccupation with the two natures of Christ to an examination of how Jesus related to the people and structures of his society. How do you understand the mission and ministry of Jesus? In what way do you view his prophetic lifestyle as normative for your own? What does it mean that he is truly God and truly human?

Beyond Professionalism in Ministry and Education

by Sara Butler, MSBT

AUTOBIOGRAPHICAL STATEMENT

Hans Hoekendijk, eminent missiologist and world ecumenist, once advised me to hurry on and finish my dissertation so that I could begin to live. I did eventually finish it **(Intercommunion in an American Perspective**, presented for a Ph.D. in systematic theology from Fordham University in 1971), and since then have been engaged in living, with my theological training serving as a background against which to reflect on the data of my pastoral experience.

My choice of serving in parish, deanery, diocesan, and congregational structures rather than in an academic setting has cut down on some kinds of theological productivity but opened the door to others. Because of my particular posture, balancing between two worlds, I have become most deeply involved in those theological questions which arise from the life of the Church today. I am keenly interested in the urgent questions of the ecumenical movement (Eucharistic sharing, interchurch marriage, women's ordination, the exercise of papal primacy) and in the redefinition of roles and responsibilities within the Roman Catholic Church (roles of women, of lay persons, of parish and diocesan councils). These topics inevitably drive one back to more general considerations of ecclesiology.

When I search out significant influences on my life and work, I come up with the following list. First, my childhood in Toledo, Ohio, where I was blessed with a well-educated and pious family and twelve years of private education with the Ursuline Sisters. I had, I now realize, an unusually rich experience of Catholic culture. Two years (1961-63) in the M.A. program at the Catholic University of America, during the heyday of pre-Vatican II enthusiasm in the Religious Education Department (under the guidance of Rev. Gerard S. Sloyan), reinforced the best of my early experience and gave me a wide and deep exposure to the theological sources of my own tradition. The post-Conciliar years of course work at Fordham (1965-67) opened up a vast, ecumenical horizon and led me to a more critical appraisal of that tradition. Teaching experience at two church-related Protestant colleges (Dickinson and The College of Wooster) gave me an invaluable window on American Christianity in its various forms and forced me to articulate the central values of Roman Catholicism. Six years in the diocese of Mobile, Alabama, as director of adult education for the Mobile deanery, gave me an indispensable introduction to the reality of the local Church.

Since 1956, all of my experiences have been most profoundly influenced by my membership in the Missionary Servants of the Most Blessed Trinity, an American congregation dedicated to the preservation of the faith, the service of the most "abandoned" in the home mission field, and the empowerment of the laity. My lived experience with sisters involved in almost every facet of Church life continually invites me to engage in that kind of theological reflection which will most surely contribute to the solution of the pastoral problems they face, illuminate the logic of the pastoral experiments they undertake, and clarify the role of "missionaries" in a changing Church.

I have kept up professionally through teaching (for the past six summers at the Catechetical and Pastoral Institute of Loyola University, New Orleans), participation in the Anglican-Roman Catholic Consultation in the U.S. (since 1973), active membership in the Catholic Theological Society of America (board member, 1977-79; chairperson for study on women in Church and society), occasional publication, and service on ad hoc committees and seminars.

Sara Butler, MSBT

Not so long ago a paper on the intersection of ministry and education might have been addressed to a group of Jesuit schoolteachers—hyphenated priests—in consideration of their particular role and witness. For "ministry" until very recently was understood to be the service rendered by ordained men, and "education" was taken to be something that happened in classrooms.

The rapid and remarkable transformation and expansion of these two terms is the concern at hand. Today, "ministry" functions as a description of almost any kind of service rendered in the name of the Lord and for the sake of the Kingdom, irrespective of priestly ordination. And "education" embraces almost any process that leads to human growth and development towards maturity, regardless of the setting in which this takes place. There is need to clarify and redefine the boundaries of these terms lest they escape all control and become too amorphous to be useful. More especially, there is need to get a handle on their interrelationship.

In some sense, all ministry may be considered a form of education, for it is directed towards human growth and development in some respect. Likewise, education can be classified as a form of ministry in so far as it constitutes a service offered in the Lord's name. But the terms are not synonymous. Who is the minister, and what do we expect from her? Who is the educator, and what is his function? What does it mean to earn a degree in "pastoral ministry"? How will the content of this degree program differ from courses leading to a degree in "religious education"? These issues become most concrete when role definitions are attempted. What is the difference between a "youth minister" and a "consultant for high school religious education"? Between a "pastoral minister" and a DRE? How can we explain the current preference for "ministry" over "education" on the part of large numbers of persons formerly dedicated to Catholic schooling? These practical questions oblige us to consider how these functions are related to each other.

If the intersection of ministry and education might have been located in the person of the priest-educator some years back, today, I would like to suggest, it might be located in the parish catechumenate. Let us suppose several candidates present themselves for admission to baptism. They are received by a small group of committed adult parishioners who will undertake to assist with their initiation into the community. One aspect of this initiation will be a kind of formal catechesis—a passing on of the inheritance of Catholic faith and practice. The context for this catechesis is a community of persons dedicated to nurturing the incipient faith of the inquirers. In telling the catechumens the Christian Story, these members of the sponsoring community lend it the flesh and blood of their own life stories. In admitting doubts and raising questions, the sponsors acknowledge the open-endedness of the faith pilgrimage. In announcing certainties, they confirm their own best insights and deepest beliefs. For their part, the catechumens share with the sponsoring group their needs, longings, questions, and hopes. As they disclose their own pain, incompleteness, and sinfulness they invite their sponsors to minister to them. This ministry is exercised by every member of the group who sincerely offers the support of faith, prayer, and friendship to the catechumens. The entire parish collaborates in this ministry as the several stages of the catechumenate are publicly celebrated during the Lenten liturgies. The process culminates in the sacramental initiation of the candidates during the Easter Vigil.

What happens in the catechumenate is **education** in that the tradition is passed on from the sponsors to the catechumens. It is not simply an "inquiry class," however, for the educational process involves the catechumens as full participants in creative reflection and dialogue. As adults, each brings along a personal history, a set of values and habits and attitudes that will enter into the process and draw the others forward. In the intimacy of a small learning community, a certain mutuality is established. The educational process is dialogical.

What happens is at the same time **ministry** insofar as the sponsors are present and available to the catechumens as believing persons, willing to engage themselves as companions in a common search for meaning, and to offer the support of their concern and prayer. This process is an expression of ministry in a still more formal sense inasmuch as it is incorporated into the public proclamation of the Word and celebration of the sacraments of initiation. The action of the parish community and, in particular, of its pastor, is an expression of the Church's ministry to its new members.

I submit that in a situation like this, education and ministry are fully integrated moments in a single process. The educational model respects the freedom and adulthood of the catechumens and encompasses them with manifestations of human caring and friendship. There is an attention to the real needs of the catechumens and an effort to walk with them in the quest for faith. In the culminating liturgy, the great themes of Christian faith are proclaimed and the catechumens are initiated into the mysteries of faith through the experience of water, oil, bread, and wine.

In proposing this example of the intersection or overlap between education and ministry, I am using the term "ministry" according to an increasingly popular conception in Roman Catholic circles. Let me stop at this point and explore further this current usage.

I have identified the "ministry" of the sponsors in the catechumenal community with their attitudes of personal interest, sincere concern, and genuine support in friendship. That is, I am suggesting that it is the presence of these attitudes that makes their activity something more than an inquiry class or a stimulating group exploration of the faith. Ministry, here, implies a posture of service which is inseparable from a particular intentionality. That intentionality, it seems to me, is one of being attentive to another in faith. It implies a desire to introduce the presence and power of God into a situation of need and to disclose God as the ever-present source of hope and strength. The minister, in this case, lends his or her own experience of God in faith to the other, supporting the other in a very personal way.

This usage of "ministry" is not identical with "**the** ministry" used as the equivalent of "the priesthood" or "the pastoral office." It refers, rather, to a style of Christian service which draws upon and seeks to give expression to the ministry of Jesus. Without excluding, certainly, a relationship to "the ministry" as a state in life or office, the understanding I speak of has more to do with a particular stance in the service of others.

Let me give an example. A friend was circulating flyers through the neighborhood to attract attendance at a "resource fair" for single parents. At the fair would be a great variety of exhibits and persons representing various agencies which stood ready to be of service to single parents. Upon entering a local grocery store, my friend was seized upon by the elderly Italian couple who were its proprietors. They called out to their daughter in the back room to come quickly. She had, they explained, just been abandoned by her husband. Her parents were sure she should be signed up for the single parents' resource fair and tried to elicit some enthusiasm from her. My friend was saddened by their lack of sensitivity. What that young woman needed was not education (the resource fair); she needed ministry. I believe the translation of that is this: this woman was in pain and needed someone to listen, to reassure her of her self-worth, to help her keep body and soul together during this extraordinary crisis. Education could come later.

My friend used the term "ministry." Why? How has this new usage crept into our vocabulary? What is its value?

I venture to say that this usage has come to us chiefly from two sources. In the first place, we receive it from Protestant Pentecostalism, via the Catholic charismatic movement. Caught up in the renewal movement, multitudes of Catholics have learned that they have "gifts" to be offered to others in the name of the Lord; multitudes have been awakened to the notion that by the power of the Spirit they are able to "minister" to the needs of others. Secondly, this vocabulary is familiar to the Clinical Pastoral Education Movement. As more and more Catholics take part in this sort of pastoral training, they begin to speak of ministry as a style of pastoral care. Henri Nouwen, coming from this experience, has probably done more than any other single person to introduce this usage of the term "ministry" to our Church. In his truly significant book, **Creative Ministry,** Nouwen expresses eloquently the need to go beyond professionalism in the services we offer as Christians.[1] He demonstrates how five areas of ministry (teaching, preaching, counseling, organizing, and celebrating) become truly ministerial when they draw upon the resources of the minister's own spiritual life.

This is the critical new point of integration represented by the term "ministry." Whatever task is undertaken in the service of others becomes ministry when it is consciously set in relation to one's personal knowledge of God, life of faith, struggle with prayer. It becomes ministry by virtue of contemplation—an attitude of attentiveness to another in which the minister comes to see how God is touching the other's life.[2]

The basic model for this style is really counseling, or what Nouwen classifies as "individual pastoral care." It is akin to spiritual direction, another recently revived ministry. On this model, the minister must be conscious that the risk of service is to lay down one's life for another. Ministry involves two moments: self-affirmation and self-denial. The minister has to believe, on the one hand, that she can bring life to a situation because she is the agent of God's loving promises. In this respect, she must be ready to take the initiative in a pastoral relationship. On the other hand, she should be prepared for rejection and must be ready to empty herself in love for the other, in witness to God's covenant love which endures through failure.

This understanding of ministry as a special quality of service rendered from the depths of a person's own faith can be expanded from the situation of individual pastoral care and extended to Christian teaching, preaching, organizing, and the leading of worship.[3] It strikes the really essential chord, namely, that ministry is rooted in that relationship with Jesus Christ which shapes the minister's own life. This relationship is what gives rise to the special intentionality which characterizes all that may be called ministry.

What has been rediscovered, what excites us in the contemporary emphasis, is nothing less than the essence of Christian ministry. Ministry is service inspired by the Spirit, according to the example of Jesus, who came not to be served but to serve and to give his life as a ransom for many (Mark 10:45). It is the service of one who is willing to lay down his life for his friends (John 15:13). Nouwen goes further by insisting that it is out of our weakness, our woundedness, that we minister most creatively.[4] Whatever else is said about ministry must touch base with this, I think. Otherwise, we have only various functions and offices within the community, subject to the manipulations of our sinfulness.

Now these considerations may seem to have wandered from the topic, namely, the nature, function, and interrelation of education and ministry. Let me attempt to line up this popular conception of ministry with our more usual frame of reference.

Most systematic reflection on ministry today takes the ministry of Jesus as its starting point. This one ministry is not discontinued after the Resurrection; rather, the Spirit of God is poured out on the whole Church, constituting it a priestly people (Acts 2:17-18; 1 Pet. 2:5-9; Rev. 1:6; 5:10). All the baptized, strengthened by the powerful presence of the Risen Lord, exercise the one ministry or service whereby the redeeming love of God is proclaimed to the world. It is this general or universal ministry which provides the context for understanding ministry as a personal stance in service which draws upon the servant's own life of faith. Such ministry encompasses works of charity and of mercy, spontaneous teaching and exhortation, leadership in prayer, and advocacy for the oppressed.

Every genuine service to one's neighbor bears witness to the sustaining and life-giving presence of the Lord. Christian ministry is, in fact, "participation in the ministry of Christ."[5]

From here, contemporary treatises on ministry generally recount the special functions or ministries enumerated in the New Testament catalogues (1 Cor. 12:28-30; Rom. 12:6-8; Eph. 4:7-12). Some were apostles, some prophets, miracle workers, healers, almsgivers, administrators, tonguespeakers, and so on. These charisms given for the service of the community were distributed throughout the Church. We do not have any precise counterparts in the Church today because these diverse ministries were eventually absorbed into the pastoral office or special Ministry, that is, the Ministry of the ordained.[6]

There is considerable interest in restoring this diversity of ministries in the life of the Church. We hear of "lay ministries" and "non-ordained ministries" and realize that the subject is not simply the universal ministry of the baptized but rather a new development, a stage somewhere between spontaneous charismatic expressions and the Ministry of the deacon, priest, and bishop. Let me complete the sketch I have begun by considering the Ministry of the ordained and accounting for the eclipse of lay ministries. Then I shall return to examine further the implication of this development.

A contemporary theology of Ministry, informed by recent biblical studies and challenged by ecumenical dialogue, takes note of the fact that we do not find in the apostolic community a replica of the ecclesiastical hierarchy we have today in the Roman Catholic Church.[7] Rather, the evolution of the offices of bishop, priest, and deacon is acknowledged to have taken place over a period of years. The "ordering" of the Church came about as a response to the needs of the community. Some aspects of ministry stand closer to the center of the community's identity, such as preaching the Word, initiating new members, celebrating the Lord's Supper, and presiding over the Church and its works.

More than simply a response to social necessity, however, the call to the special Ministry, a service of leadership at the heart of the community, has always been linked to the priesthood of Christ (which is its source and its model) and to the call of the Twelve. Ordination is the Church's sacramentalization of a charism bestowed by God. In the Roman Catholic theological tradition, apostolic succession is a way of laying claim to this vocation as God-given and authentically connected with the origins of the Church.

It is important to observe that in the evolution of the special Ministry over the first three centuries, most of the spontaneous charismatic gifts were absorbed into the formal structure of pastoral office.[8] By the fourth century, the dichotomy between clergy and laity became increasingly evident, and because the exercise of the various ministries was subject to the authority of the clergy, it appeared that the clergy alone were responsible for ministerial initiatives. They could redistribute tasks to others, but these tasks belonged to them by right. In the extreme form of papal theology it was taught that all authority for ministry was held by the pope, who, as Peter's successor, was heir to the power of the keys and the Vicar of Christ. According to this view, bishops were understood to participate in the ministry of the pope, while priests and deacons were understood to participate in the ministry of the bishops. Ministry, then, came to be viewed as something delegated from on high rather than as a fundamental expression of Christian faith and witness. This theology of ministry reached its logical conclusion in the definition of the lay apostolate as "the participation of the laity in the mission of the hierarchy."[9]

A theology of the laity developed during the 1930s, 40s, and 50s,[10] and this extreme clericalism was thrown into reverse. The Second Vatican Council officially taught that membership in the Church through baptism established a fundamental equality; that persons in positions of leadership were placed at the service of the community; that the Holy Spirit would gift and grace all members of the Church in unique ways for the sake of the entire community.[11]

The reversal now in process is not just a matter of promoting the "apostolate of the laity," as Bernard Cooke points out.[12] Quite the contrary, it is a matter of recognizing the ministry of the Christian community as a whole. All Christians, including those who are also ordained, participate in the corporate ministry of the Church by reason of baptism. The prophetic Spirit works throughout the members, calling forth a variety of ministries for the building of the Body. What is needed now, it has been argued, is some formal recognition of these diverse charisms which enrich the Church, so that the notion that all ministerial initiative belongs exclusively to the ordained will be corrected.

We come back to a consideration of the prospect of multiplying formally recognized but non-ordained ministries. This, of course, is more than just a prospect. The "motu proprio" **Ministeria quaedam** of 1972 replaced the tonsure and minor orders with the ministries of reader (or lector) and acolyte. Persons "instituted" or "installed" into these ministries are not clerics. They are the ordinary ministers in the functions they perform. This is neither the universal ministry of all the baptized nor the special Ministry of deacon, priest, and bishop. It is, rather, ecclesial recognition that a given person has received a particular gift for service; it is the consecration of that person's gift in a relatively stable role for the service of the local Church. Such public recognition presumes a certain level of competence in the performance of the ministerial function. Through this installation, the Church makes a commitment to the minister and has the right to require accountability with respect to the exercise of this function.[13]

Two other "ministries" (in this sense) have been recommended by the bishops of the United States: the ministry of catechist and the ministry of music.[14] It is not clear that women would be prevented from liturgical installation into these ministries. The exclusion of women from the ministries of reader and acolyte explains why to date the only men installed into these functions in this formal way are almost exclusively candidates for the permanent diaconate and for the priesthood.

One has the lingering suspicion that the creation of non-ordained ministries arises out of the need to prove that many roles in the Church's life are open to women—roles for which a natural resemblance to Jesus Christ is not required![15] Again, one wonders whether the elaboration of these roles is not a subtle way of bringing gifted persons under ecclesiastical control. One may ask whether and to what extent the formal institution of diverse ministries in the Church will contribute to its declericalization. It is just possible that adding to the ranks of ministers may only develop a new class of super-Christians.

On the other hand, the liturgical installation of competent persons gifted and called by the community for the exercise of certain ministries in the Church has much to commend it. It is far more appropriate, in my opinion, than the rather common form of admission to ministry that comes by way of a juridical delegation of authority, that is, by episcopal mandate.[16] The Church publicly authorizes a competent person to function on its behalf. This person is chosen on the basis of proven ability or leadership in some area of ministry. This witness of this life, already acknowledged by its "success" in the community, is then drawn formally into the life and structure of the Church. This pattern, I believe, discloses the inner meaning of ordination: a person who has demonstrated spiritual leadership is acknowledged by the community and inserted into the inner circle of its life through a liturgical celebration.

The restoration of the permanent diaconate has given us direct experience of this understanding of ordination. Men recommended by the community on the basis of a charism already exercised are called forth, provided with further training and formation, and then authorized by the Church to function in a stable and public fashion. Their spontaneous expressions of ministry are identified as belonging to the ministry of Christ and his Church through ordination. **Installation** into a lay ministry has very much the same character but is appropriate for more specialized functions or services not so intimately related to the Ministry of Word and Sacrament.

What comes to light is a spectrum of ministry in the Church, ranging from the charismatic ministries of the baptized, through the ecclesially recognized lay ministries, to the orders of deacon, priest, and bishop. All participate in the one ministry of Christ, but, according to the call each receives, they participate with varying degrees of intensity, comprehensiveness, and authority. This spectrum of ministry parallels a spectrum of sacramentality, whereby the wholesome, human activities of every day (eating together, loving, forgiving, supporting, healing, and so on) are seen to exist on a continuum with and find their full expression in the sacraments of the Church. We may say, with Bernard Cooke, that the ordained Ministry functions as a "sacrament" within the sacramentality of the Church as a whole.[17]

To return to my initial point, the essential requirement for ministry, however exercised, is that the minister be a person of faith, a person rooted in Christ and attentive to his Spirit. The current reassessment of ministry highlights this, if nothing else. Pastoral office, with its analogous expressions, is effective and compelling to the extent that the officer has a genuine charism and is personally engaged in the imitation of the ministry of Christ.

Let me turn back now to the subject of education. I have proposed that the parish catechumenate might serve as an example of the intersection between ministry and education. In suggesting this I make several presuppositions which I would like to surface.[18] In the first place, I regard education as a process which leads to human growth and development towards maturity. Second, I accept as primary a socialization model of education. The handing-on of the wisdom and culture of a community is of the essence of education. The most comprehensive context for this handing-on is the society into which the person is introduced. This is inevitably the model in the case of a child whose learning comes not only from doing but from the response (approval/disapproval) of significant others in his or her life. Third, I choose the catechumenate because it is a model of adult education. Unlike the child, the adult is capable of critical reflection and independent evaluation. The adult is in a position to question the inherited wisdom because life experience has equipped her with personal criteria of "what is so" and "how things are." The education by socialization that encompasses the life of a child is gradually confronted by the probings and personal discoveries of the young adult.

What is true of education in general is true of religious education and catechesis. The critical moment comes when the learner's "Why?" represents not a plea for more information but a challenge to the received tradition. As Freire has convinced us, education is an instrument of oppression when this "Why?" is ignored or the questioner reprimanded.[19] A "banking" concept of education is destructive of human growth and repressive to human freedom. It leads not to maturity but to the internalization of inadequacy. If, on the other hand, the teacher accepts the "Why?" and joins in a search for the truth of the matter, patiently entering into the experience of the learner who poses the question, then education becomes an experience of liberation. The creativity of the learner is released; a partnership is formed; the dialogue between the learner's experience and the world of information and interpretation inherited from the society begins, and no one can know its outcome.

Just as adult baptism stands as the norm for our understanding of the nature of this sacrament, so adult education is normative for our understanding of the true potential and final goal of the educational process. In both instances, the adult is invited to responsible, personal participation. The experience of faith, like the experience of insight, cannot be feigned. The person must be grasped individually and brought to a point of enlightenment or conversion. The socialization process is unable to supply this radically personal step.

On the other side of the coin, I am convinced that children and youth need to have the wisdom of the tradition, the faith of their ancestors, confidently and boldly proclaimed. Those who have reached a certain maturity owe the young at least this much: some certainties with which to face the world and all its ambiguities. Critical reflection must be awakened and sustained, but it is not the principal pedagogy for the young where the fundamental truths of our lives are concerned.

The inevitable tension between "socialization" and "critical reflection" as models of education mirrors the tension that exists in the area of ministry.

The leadership of the special Ministry tends to assume the stewardship of the tradition; that, in fact, is one of its central roles. The spontaneous outpouring of the charismatic ministry, on the other hand, tends to spring more directly from experience (including personal religious experience). Charismatic ministry not only supports, it also challenges the established Ministry. Taken from an even larger perspective, we note today that the Church as institution or social entity lives in tension with the Church of the grassroots, that is, with the various expressions of local community (e.g., the **communidades eclesiales de base**) which are renewing the Church "from below."[20]

At the outset of this paper I suggested that all ministry can in some respect be considered a form of education, for ministry, too, is service on behalf of human wholeness. If education entails the enablement of persons to confront and interact creatively with life, then ministry has much the same goal. Education as socialization provides a context of community tradition for the individual's search for meaning. Education as liberation facilitates the dialogue with reality in which a person can come to full potential as creator of her own destiny.

It is probably more adequate, however, to view education as a form of ministry. The scope of what we are calling ministry includes all that leads to human growth and wholeness, not just the dimension of life properly addressed by education. This larger scope I take to include all the brokenness of life: physical pain,

emotional pain, sin, hunger and thirst, loneliness, alienation, powerlessness, poverty, confusion, injustice, death. The Christian
minister approaches these situations with honesty and faith, proclaiming the Good News of God's fidelity and announcing the
triumph of the Cross. This ministry, whose source is the Spirit but
whose agent is himself wounded and incomplete, is addressed to
the whole person, to communities, even to systems.

It appears to me that ministry is the umbrella term under
which true Christian education falls. Education is ministry under
the specific formality of proclamation, reflection, clarification, and
integration of understanding. It has to do most properly with the
search for truth and wisdom. Pedagogy is, of course, not limited to
the classroom and the teacher-pupil relationship. It does, however,
concern itself with that dialogue with reality which eventuates in
knowledge. While it may not ignore the dimensions of community
and service,[21] these are not its immediate objects.

Ministry, the broader category, seeks to introduce the presence
and power of God into a concrete human situation of need. This
need may be particular to some group of persons (youth, the elderly, the divorced, single people, and so on) or it may be the
universal needs of the human heart: to be known, to be loved, to be
saved from alienation and sin. Ministry moves in with confidence
born of God's Spirit, and trepidation born of our own failings.
Comforting, challenging, healing, nurturing, the Christian minister
seeks to witness to the reconciliation God has effected in Jesus
Christ our Lord.

Why are graduate students asking for preparation for pastoral
ministry? What does this title suggest to them in addition to, or as
distinct from, a degree in religious education? I believe the difference lies in the assimilation of this term to the model of individual
pastoral care. What attracts is the suggestion that a commitment to
interpersonal relationships on the level of ultimate meaning is
going to be demanded. Somehow, courses in ministry require a
kind of reflection or a process of theologizing that virtually demand
the integration of the minister's personal experience with the
ministry offered.[22] Ministry, more than education, calls to mind a
model of mutuality: in our common humanity we stand before the
mystery of life and the mystery of God. Ministry, more than education, suggests the presence and support of the community, especially the peer group. It explicitly invites the sharing of prayer and

of faith within the group. Ministry, more than education, evokes the idea of appealing to memory and experience-based learning, such as the review of life stories, journal-keeping, and action-reflection techniques. Ministry, more than education, has as its objective wholeness and holiness which the Gospel promises— whether this be the transformation of lives or of systems. Finally, ministry, more than education, holds out the promise that the one who serves will be molded by her service into the likeness of Jesus who laid down his life for others. Granted, the model of adult education which incorporates Freire's theory very generally introduces the educator into the same series of relationships. But when this happens, the educator inevitably refers to the experience as "ministry."

NOTES

1. Henri J. M. Nouwen, **Creative Ministry** (New York: Doubleday, 1971).

2. Ibid., p. 61.

3. It is becoming evident that the ministry of organizing politically for the cause of social justice does not find a place so easily when this model predominates. This is one of its major weaknesses, in my opinion.

4. Nouwen, pp. 45-65. See also Henri Nouwen, **The Wounded Healer** (New York: Doubleday, 1972).

5. Bernard Cooke, in **Ministry to Word and Sacraments** (Philadelphia: Fortress, 1976), discusses this on p. 197.

6. I have chosen to adopt the usage of the Lutheran-Roman Catholic Consultation: lower case for the ministry of the whole Church and upper case for the special Ministry. See **Lutherans and Catholics in Dialogue IV: Eucharist and Ministry** (Washington, D.C.: U.S.C.C., 1970), p. 9.

7. Raymond E. Brown, **Priest and Bishop** (New York: Paulist, 1970) and **Biblical Reflections on Crises Facing the Church** (New York: Paulist, 1975), pp. 52-55. The most thorough contemporary study is that of Bernard Cooke, cited in note 5.

8. This development is traced by Cooke (chapters 2 and 3) and commented on, pp. 193-214. A brief recapitulation of this evolution is also found in **Study Text III: Ministries in the Church** (Washington, D.C.: U.S.C.C., 1974), pp. 17-21.

9. This notion was popular with Pius XI and Pius XII. See, for example, Pius XII, "Allocution to Italian Catholic Action," Sept. 4, 1940: **AAS** 32 (1940), 362. See also D. J. Geaney, "Catholic Action," **New Catholic Encyclopedia** 3 (New York: McGraw-Hill, 1967), 262-263.

10. Theological expression was given to this development by the classic work of Yves Congar, **Lay People in the Church** (Westminster, Md.: Newman, 1965).

11. See especially **Lumen Gentium,** arts. 30-38.

12. Cooke, p. 203.

13. **Origins** (vol. 8) carried the report "Ministries and the Local Church: Conclusions of an Asian Colloquium on Ministries" in which the following position was taken:

> Ministries apply more properly to those services which church members undertake with a certain stability and exercise on a sufficiently broad basis, thus sharing formally in the Church's responsibility to signify the presence to men [sic] of Christ's saving action. All such ministries must be recognized by the community and authenticated by it in the person of its leader. Thus, every service and ministry of the church suppose a charism but not every charism blossoms into a ministry. (pp. 133-34)

14. These are described in **Study Text III,** pp. 48-50.

15. See the report of the Pastoral Commission of the Sacred Congregation for the Evangelization of Peoples, "The Role of Women in Evangelization," **Origins** 5 (April 2, 1976), 702-707, for the source of this concern.

16. Joseph Komonchak provides a very thorough critique of this practice in his excellent study, "The Permanent Diaconate and the Variety of Ministries in the Church," **Proceedings, Permanent Diaconate Directors' Meeting** (Washington, D.C.: U.S.C.C., 1977). He argues that admission to ministry by way of "delegation of authority" (such as is the pattern where women and some lay men are authorized to administer parishes and carry out all the functions of deacons) goes contrary to the Second Vatican Council's conception of the sacrament of orders.

17. Cooke, pp. 643-49.

18. I am greatly indebted to the stimulating essays produced for an earlier symposium at Boston College, **Foundations of Religious Education,** edited by Padraic O'Hare (New York: Paulist, 1978). I found Berard Marthaler's contribution especially congenial. With Francoise Darcy-Berube, I believe this socialization model must be constantly corrected—where adults are concerned—with the "shared praxis" approach proposed by Thomas H. Groome.

19. Paulo Freire, **Pedagogy of the Oppressed** (New York: Seabury, 1973).

20. See, for instance, the cautionary note in the Apostolic Exhortation **Evangelii Nuntiandi** (December 8, 1975), art. 58.

21. These dimensions of the educational task are given prominence in the pastoral message of the National Conference of Catholic Bishops, **To Teach as Jesus Did** (Washington, D.C.: U.S.C.C., 1973).

22. This theme which I have developed has been (I discover) very well set forth by Colin MacDonald, executive director of the U.S. bishops' Committee on Priestly Life and Ministry. See "The Future of Ministry," **Origins** 8 (October 5, 1978), 248-53.

QUESTIONS FOR DISCUSSION

1) Butler locates the intersection of ministry and education in the parish catechumenate. Has the catechumenate, in your experience, proved to be such a juncture? Are you aware of other programs and situations in which ministry and education intersect?

2) How would you go about educating people regarding the changing views of ministry so that those who were once taught that their apostolate was to participate in the mission of the hierarchy might come to recognize the "corporate ministry of the Church by reason of baptism"?

3) Butler notes that the contemporary recognition and formal institution of diverse ministries might merely increase clericalism and lead to a class of "super-Christians." Nevertheless, she applauds this process, holding it to be more appropriate than the more common form of admission to ministry by episcopal mandate. What do you see to be the advantages and disadvantages of multiplying non-ordained ministries?

4) "The essential requirement for ministry—however exercised—is that the minister be a person of faith, a person rooted in Christ and attentive to his Spirit." By what criteria is one judged to be (or not to be) a "person of faith"? Who decides this? What is the decision-making process for such a judgment?

5) While initially making the hypothesis that, on the one hand, all ministry may be considered a form of education, yet, on the other hand, education may be classified as a form of ministry, Butler ultimately concludes that "ministry is the umbrella term under which true Christian education falls." Do you agree with her classification? Might not education, which has a meaning beyond a strictly ecclesiastical context, enhance the practice of various ministries insofar as it helps people to "reconstruct" their experience, that is, to reflect on and rethink what has happened in their lives?

6) Butler holds that ministry, more than education, involves a
model of mutuality, suggests communal support and sharing,
and is oriented toward gospel wholeness and holiness. What
educational models might embody these same characteristics?

7) As people are being trained for ministry today by means of the
skills of pastoral care, should they not also be taught some of the
skills of teaching? Is there any ministry that does not have an
educational component?

Tradition and Modernity: Managerial Images of Ministry in Protestant Church Education, 1900-1920

by Robert Wood Lynn

AUTOBIOGRAPHICAL STATEMENT

"Are you going into the ministry or Christian education?" That question, which an older student asked me on my first day at Yale Divinity School in the late 1940s, reverberated in my thoughts as I prepared for the Boston College symposium. Of course it was a silly question with a false either/or flavor.

Still it made sense in 1948 to a Presbyterian who had long been accustomed to the usual arrangements of a Protestant congregation. In the little Wyoming church where I was baptized, the Sunday school and the congregation which gathered for worship at eleven o'clock on the Sabbath seemed to exist in different worlds. If the Sunday school proved to be the dominant symbol of education, then "ministry" belonged to the congregation. My later experience as an infantry soldier in World War II and as an undergraduate at Princeton University had not erased a child's impression of the spiritual distance between those two intertwined institutions. That early experience helped me, therefore, to understand the otherwise obscure logic of the query about the choice of either "ministry" or "education."

As it turned out, ironically enough, I chose both. After Yale my first assignment was to be a "minister of education" in a large, sprawling church in Denver, Colorado. Despite the excitement of the post-World War II years in theology, we made little progress in the 1950s in thinking through the theological connection between ministry and education. It might have been different had we pressed the line of inquiry opened up by James D. Smart in his work, **The Teaching Ministry of the Church.**[1] Later on in my essay,

97

I will have more to say about the significance of this now largely forgotten book.

For better or worse (worse, in my judgment), Smart's promising beginnings were not criticized or developed in any systematic way in the 1960s. During that tumultuous decade the word "ministry" was attached to all manner of activity. Our failure to refine the meaning of the vague phrase, "the ministry of education," went unnoticed amidst the distractions of an expanding array of fashionable new forms of ministry. In the luxury of retrospective wisdom, I wish that I had concentrated more consistently in the 1960s on the task of clarifying the relation between ministry and education. Still these years yielded a full harvest of riches: I enjoyed the honor of teaching at Union Theological Seminary in New York City, where I received a doctorate in 1962; likewise, I found myself thrust into the exciting work of exploring the history of Christian **paideia** in America. That gift, in turn, brought a new sense of appreciation for what Catholics and Protestants might learn from and with each other about education.

In that spirit I offered the following reflection at the November gathering to a predominantly Catholic audience as a momentary diversion from its current preoccupations. At first glance this modest tale may appear to have little to teach contemporary Catholic educators. But the subsequent discussion at the Boston College symposium convinced me that many Catholics, as well as Protestants, are also struggling with the fundamental problem which is touched upon in these pages. Whatever our differences, we may discover a new unity in the common endeavor to face up to the issue of tradition and modernity.

Robert Wood Lynn

The formative influence of the community on its members is most constantly active in its deliberate endeavor to educate each new generation of individuals so as to make them in its own image. The structure of every society is based on the written or unwritten laws which bind it and its members. Therefore, education in any human community (be it a family, a social class, a profession, or some wide complex such as a race or a state) is the direct expression of its active awareness of a **standard**.[2]

—Werner Jaeger,
Paideia: The Ideals of Greek Culture

If the liberal Protestants claimed the right to a critical use of tradition, they were in principle claiming nothing more than did Luther and Calvin; Protestantism was by nature revisionary from the first. And when Troeltsch objects that the way one of his conservative opponents has argued would result in confining every man to the religion in which he was born, he is simply echoing a sentiment we have found already in Calvin. But there is a difference. While there is no novelty in the call, as such, for reappraisal of tradition, the problem has now shifted (so to say) from the inside to the outside: it is not so much that tradition itself has been corrupted by the infidelity of the church as that the church's tradition in the modern world has become insecure. The problem, for the liberal, is no longer "Scripture and tradition" but "tradition (including Scripture) and modernity."[3]

—B. A. Gerrish,
Tradition and the Modern World

In our own time-possessed way, we Americans enjoy the turning of the decades. The flip of the calendar from 1979 to 1980 brings on easy slogans about the sins of the past ten years—the "Me Decade," for instance—and predictions of the shape of things to come. The pundits have already made a cliché of the 1980s. But these occasions can also stir us to think freshly about the sweep of history and to rediscover the fundamental issues that must be dealt with in the days ahead. If I am at all correct in my musings about the past and the immediate future, the theme of this symposium embodies one of the crucial challenges for Christian educators in the 1980s.

In preparing these thoughts about "Ministry and Education," my mind kept straying to two unlikely sources of illumination. Instead of focusing upon some obvious point of departure such as Bernard Cooke's remarkable investigation of **Ministry to Word and Sacraments,**[4] I have been prompted to begin with the two works cited at the outset, neither of which has a direct bearing upon the topic of our conversation. Yet these texts, each in its own way, suggest an approach into the heart of the matter.

Let us start with Werner Jaeger and his ruminations about the evolution of **paideia** in the life of ancient Greece. The theme of this magisterial accomplishment, enunciated above in a bare, almost platitudinous form, takes on rich meaning in the course of his leisurely examination of different Greek epochs. That same motif would have figured prominently in his projected history of **paideia** in the early Christian era, had he ever been able to complete it. In any event Jaeger's insight is just as pertinent for the historians of Christian education as it was in his own work.

One way of ferreting out the **actual** norms governing church life in any period is to examine the array of arguments about ministry in that time. Who is considered qualified to minister? Only the pious, or the orthodox or the learned? What is meant by "learned"—the "Christian gentleman" for instance, or the "modern professional"? In every age there are certain reigning images of ministry. These definitions of ministry represent a peculiarly potent source of educationally relevant standards. In sum, the histories of ministry and of church education are inextricably interwoven with each other. We do not discern one strand without seeing the other.

It is no accident, therefore, that there is neither an adequate account of American **paideia** nor a comprehensive analysis of the changing conceptions of ministry in this country. The lack of a serious history of Christian education in the United States is, alas, painfully self-evident. And while Bernard Cooke included some marvelously suggestive historical interpretations of images of ministry in his recent book, he chose to range far beyond the American scene.

Without these foundational works in place, I cannot construct the scaffold of an argument that is centered around a series of informed generalizations about the impact of changing notions of ministry upon church education. My best alternative is to concentrate upon one episode in that tangled history of American Protestant education and ministry. By attending to one small chapter in the larger story, we might be able to sense the possibilities of that unwritten history.

The episode focus is the introduction in the early 1900s of a new form of ministry—the Director of Religious Education. For a brief, tantalizing interlude, the acronym "DRE" stood for a promising blend of a revised **tradition** and relevant **modernity.** In a few decades, however, the glamor of that new post faded away, forgotten or repressed amidst sour disappointments about misplaced hopes. Of course, the problem of "tradition and modernity" (B. A. Gerrish's phrase in the citation noted at the beginning) is with us still. Perhaps we can learn a thing or two from the struggles of our predecessors.

I. The Educator as Manager

It seemed to happen overnight. In 1909 a variety of large churches moved almost simultaneously to hire full-time, paid workers as Directors of Religious Education. The idea took hold, and by 1914 there were enough of these new professionals to form a respectably large national association. Just a decade later there were hundreds of newly minted "DREs" graduating from the seminaries each year.

The swift emergence of this new form of ministry surprised even its most enthusiastic boosters. When pressed to explain this startling phenomenon, they tended to point to a set of idealistic reasons. For instance, one of the movement's first interpreters cited the following reasons:

> (a) A conviction of the need of more intensive work on the part of the church in order that young people might be better instructed in Christian truth and more adequately trained for Christian service. (b) The changes taking place in religious thought by reason of the advance in scientific knowledge, changes which affected profoundly the methods of psychology, pedagogy, Bible study, sociology, and theology. (c) The changes in social life, both rural and urban, demanding that the church should adjust itself to new conditions in order to become more efficient. (d) A sense of the strategic opportunity presented by the presence of young people in the Sunday schools and Young People's societies, and the recognition that this opportunity was not being utilized to the full. (e) The neglect of moral and religious training by other institutions, such as the home and the day school.[5]

While all of these factors doubtless played some part in the rise of the DREs, I suspect there were also other forces at work. The affluent congregations which could afford to risk this innovation reaped the benefits of an expanding economy. For the first time in the life of most of these churches there was ample capital to underwrite new ventures. The comforting presence of that money made it possible for pastors and lay leaders to confront one of their major problems—an increasingly complex parish life. The minister desperately needed help to bring some order out of the bewildering profusion of Sunday school activities for persons of all ages, as well as the expanding empire of youth programs. For better or worse the white, middle-class, Protestant pastor in late Victorian America presided over a veritable organizational explosion in the life of the congregation. In addition to the youth groups mentioned above (Christian Endeavor and its various denominational imitators), the parish included new women's groups of all kinds, societies for men and a host of other agencies. The one-person church staff was no longer enough.

The creation of the DRE post represented a practical response to a growingly critical situation. From the outset, therefore, the director was perceived as an assistant to the pastor. In exercising a specialized ministry which was legitimate in its own sphere, the director could never afford to forget who was in charge. That point was made ever so delicately in one of the first articles on this new work: "While both pastor and director are alike servants and executives of the church, the pastor is the unifying and administrative head of all its work, and the director is the specially trained director of a single department."[6]

There were ample reasons to be concerned about possible strains between pastor and director. The old rivalries between the Sunday school and the congregations could easily surface in their relation. The lay-clerical distinction was also often present: in the early decades of the century the DRE was usually a layperson in contrast to the ordained cleric. Then, too, men held a monopoly upon the pastorates while the directorship provided women their first opportunity as full-time paid church workers. But the most worrisome source of potential friction resided in the differences of their respective modes of ministry. The pastor's ministry through Word and sacraments embodied the continuity of venerable tradition; meanwhile the DRE was supposed to represent modernity at its best—the competent, trained manager.

The last point is worthy of special emphasis. Make no mistake about it. The managerial image of ministry was implanted on almost every page of the early twentieth century literature about the Director of Religious Education. In any list of responsibilities the imperatives of organization-building come first, while teaching represents a lesser claim. To wit: "A director should be a good organizer, a good executive, a good teacher, and an enthusiast who is capable of inspiring others."[7]

All of these sources of possible conflict did afflict the relations between pastors and directors. Indeed, the tension would have been ever more marked if there had not been some gradual modification of the interpretation of the work of the pastor, especially among those in the liberal Protestant denominations. The same ethos which shaped the first definitions of the role of the DRE also affected the evolving normative understanding of the pastoral office.

That subtle alteration is clearly evident in the thinking of William Rainey Harper. For all of his fabled brilliance as founding president of the University of Chicago, as biblical teacher and scholarly popularizer, and as architect of the Religious Education Association, Harper remains a shadowy figure, largely unknown to later generations of American Christians. Outside of the precincts of the University of Chicago where the mention of his name still evokes filial piety, few people remember him for what he was—an extraordinarily astute observer who could identify emerging trends and thereby anticipate the shape of the future. Consider, for a moment, his discerning comments about the nature of modern ministry and the consequent responsibilities of theological seminaries. In a short essay, written in the waning months of the nineteenth century, he managed to foresee most of the seminary curricular reforms which have been rediscovered in every decade since then.

Harper was sharply critical of both Protestant ministers and the seminaries which had failed to educate them:

> It is undoubtedly true that the other professions are relatively more attractive in these modern times. This is so not only because they offer better opportunities for acquiring wealth, but also because the general influence of the minister, even when successful, has diminished, while that of the successful practitioner in law or medicine, not to speak of other professions, has greatly increased.[8]

This decline in influence, in his view, was partly due to the way in which ministers have been admitted in the profession "without adequate preparation or education. . . . It is a strange contradiction that in proportion as the requirements for entrance into other professions have gradually been elevated, in that same proportion seemingly the requirements for admission to the clerical profession have been lowered."[9] Moreover, the seminaries had accelerated the descent into mediocrity by their obstinate refusal to acknowledge the changes that were transforming the daily life of the Protestant minister. The outward manifestation of this resistance was the unchanging character of the seminaries' course of studies. "So far as I know," Harper declared, "the only professional curriculum which is essentially the same as it was fifty years ago is that of the theological seminary."[10]

Yet the "readjustment" of that curriculum could only take place after one had carefully observed the modern, "efficient" minister at work. The old curriculum may have offered adequate preparation for those ministers who focused upon the ministry of the Word and whose life, therefore, oscillated between the study and the pulpit. But the ministry was no longer a study-centered profession, any more than the law or medicine were. And so Harper was impatient to move beyond the preoccupations of yesterday:

> Let us teach that the minister's work is not merely that of preaching. Nine-tenths of the seminary work is based upon this idea. As a matter of fact, preaching should not constitute one-tenth of his work. What the minister says out of the pulpit is more important than what he says in it. We do not stand in need of preaching, as men once did; not because we are better, but because the agencies for preaching have been so multiplied; the daily papers, the magazines, the books, lecture courses, and even the theater, all furnish sermons—some of them vastly better than any we hear preached from the pulpit. The minister should recognize this fact, and by personal hand-to-hand work drive home the application of these sermons.[11]

The "personal hand-to-hand" application of society's sermons could best be accomplished through a network of organizations, some of which were church-centered and others that served the interests of the larger community. "More efficient administration," "better organization"—these were some of Harper's favorite admonitions to the clergy of his time:

> The minister must be an organizer. Let us teach him in the seminary how to organize and what to organize; and in this work of organization, of using to the best advantage every man and woman within his reach, will be found the best method of doing work in behalf of our civic institutions.[12]

While this peroration doubtless reflected his well-known penchant for order and structure,[13] it was also a forceful reminder of the changing shape of the ministry in Victorian America. If their work was to be effective, then ministers could no longer automatically rely upon the pastoral style of earlier generations—Jonathan Edwards, for instance, in the 1740s, or a Methodist circuit-rider later in the eighteenth century. As I indicated earlier, the organizational expansion of the 1880s and 1890s changed the face of the parish and the life of the minister. The new pastor's role was quite different from that of previous decades. The minister as local theologian was not as important as the role of the minister to ministers, the "general" who orders the army of the Lord forward into attack. In short, the ideal of the "pastoral director" arrived long before H. Richard Niebuhr popularized that phrase in the 1950s. Washington Gladden, the famed Congregational pastor of Columbus, Ohio, and an early exponent of the Social Gospel, put it ever so well when he wrote in 1898:

> New occasions are constantly teaching the minister of Christ new duties. His position in the church has greatly changed, and the functions he is called upon to perform are quite unlike those which were assigned to ministers in the first half of the century. The American college president of fifty years ago was the principal teacher of his college; today he rarely engages in the work of teaching. His work is mainly that of organization and administration. The change which has taken place in the function of the pastor is not so radical, but is considerable. The largest and most difficult part of his work today consists of enlisting and directing the activities of the church.[14]

The new pastor was not primarily the preacher and administrator of the sacraments envisioned by the confessional bases of many denominations. A working knowledge of Greek and Hebrew (rarely attained at that), the ability to excel in closely reasoned theological debate in addresses and sermons were considered less significant than the capacity to organize a Sunday school, to work with the women's auxiliaries, to inspire missionary interest and giving, and to build denominational loyalty. In short, the resulting portrait of the "effective" pastor bore a suspicious resemblance to the idealized DRE who should be—according to the profile which I quoted a few paragraphs ago—"a good organizer, a good executive, a good teacher, and an enthusiast who is capable of inspiring others."

I do not claim, of course, that William Rainey Harper spoke for a majority of Protestants, or that even a significant minority subscribed to the managerial interpretation of ministry. But in all likelihood both Harper and the other enthusiasts for the Director of Religious Education did reflect the views of a small but increasingly influential band of intellectuals. A generation of academics and up-to-date professionals who came into power in the 1890s and 1900s accepted the challenge of helping America move beyond reliance upon the outmoded folkways of an agrarian past and toward a confrontation of the problems inherent in an impersonal advanced industrial society. "What had emerged by the war years [World War I]," Robert H. Wiebe wrote in his persuasive interpretation of **The Search for Order,** "was an important segment of the population . . . acting from common assumptions and speaking a common language. A bureaucratic orientation now defined a basic part of the nation's discourse. The values of continuity and regularity, functionality and rationality, administration and management set the forms of problems and outlined their alternative solutions."[15] Harper and company were clearly part of that "new middle class."[16]

II. A Failure of Vision

In the early, halcyon days of the DRE boom, its proponents entertained ambitious visions of a greater future. No less a person than George Albert Coe of Union Theological Seminary (NYC) foresaw the time when denominations would "put the training of its directors of religious education upon a footing corresponding to the best practice in the preparation of superintendents of public education."[17] "The Ministry is to become differentiated," he went on to declare, "into at least three specialties, the pastorate, missionary service, and education, and each will require, say, three years of training governed strictly by the foresight of the particular functions of each."[18] Others were equally confident about the lustrous promise of this new profession.

But that envisioned future never did arrive. Shortly after World War I, and barely a decade after the first crop of DREs had been hired, there were signs that not all was well in Zion. Too often congregations hired fledgling directors with little or no advanced professional training. Moreover, the available training programs were of varying quality, and only a handful of the schools held out for the standards advocated by Coe and his fellow leaders. Then came the 1930s and the worst economic depression in the country's history. That season of disaster dealt a devastating blow to the profession, for the DRE as the last hired member of the staff was often the first one fired. The movement was not even able to regain its momentum in the comparatively easy years of religious and economic prosperity in the post-World War II era. During the 1950s and 1960s some church educators advocated a change of nomenclature as a way of renewing the profession. But the shift from "Director of Religious Education" to "Minister of Christian Education" was little more than a cosmetic gambit. The reality remained much the same: despite the best efforts of some able DREs or ministers of education, these educators as a group have not yet achieved the cohesion of a serious professional association or the goal of parity with other ministers.

What went awry? The full answer to that question lies buried in a tangle of convoluted factors which are still not identified, much less understood. Any satisfactory response will involve references to the economics of Protestant congregations, status differences between men and women, as well as between ordained and lay folk, and other complex matters. For the moment I am content with a **partial** answer. The movement floundered in part because of its inability to grasp a sufficiently comprehensive and compelling interpretation of ministry. Although the managerial image of ministry provided direction and esprit for a while during the early decades of the century, it did not help the church educators maintain their momentum amidst the economic and theological crises of the 1930s and 1940s. Or, to state the point in a slightly different way, the bureaucratic virtues of functionality and efficiency may be necessary in large-scale organizations, but they are hardly sufficient sources of motivation and commitment for a church over an extended period of time. If my historical hunch is at all correct, this limited perception of the nature of ministry represented a far more serious problem than all of the economic calamities and status ills that beset Protestant church education in the first half of the twentieth century. In hindsight one wonders why more post-liberal educational theorists of the last thirty years (including me!) did not pay sustained attention to this failure of vision. Only James D. Smart dealt with the problem in a systematic fashion. A Barthian by conviction and an Old Testament scholar by training, Smart served as the architect of the Presbyterian "Faith and Life Curriculum," the most successful of the post-World War II ventures in denominational curriculum. After he had completed his assignment and had returned to his Canadian pulpit, he wrote **The Teaching Ministry of the Church.** Although this work was not as profound or

as lasting a contribution to church education theory as C. Ellis
Nelson's later essay, **Where Faith Begins,**[19] it remains the one
Protestant book out of the last quarter of a century in which the
author grappled with the themes of our November symposium.

As a disciple of Karl Barth, Smart was intent upon recovering
the ministry of the Word as the decisive clue to church education.
Preaching and teaching belong together; preaching brings us to
Christ while teaching builds us up in Christ. Any attempt to di-
vorce **kerygma** and **didache** will finally prove destructive to the
church's ministry in education. "The whole church educates,"[20]
not just a few professionals. The inherent unity of preaching and
teaching, he believed, would eventually enable North American
Protestants to reduce the chasm between congregation and Sunday
school, pastor and minister of education. The way was now open
(1954) toward a new era in Christian education. By recovering the
essential thread of church **tradition,** the Protestant educational
theorists of the last half of the twentieth century would be able to
sort out the truth and falsity implicit in contemporary forms of
knowledge. No longer need the Christian educator be a hostage to
the pretensions of **modernity.**

Twenty-five years later, **The Teaching Ministry of the Church**
appears somewhat less convincing than it did in the early 1950s
when the neo-orthodox flood tide of confidence had reached its
highest mark. Today, for example, few of us can rest content with
Smart's way of dealing with the work of the latter-day heirs of the
Enlightenment. A careful rereading of his text reveals that he wres-
tled with only one consequence of the Enlightenment—the
historical-critical study of the Bible. But what of those other modern disciples of thought, especially those perspectives generated in
the second wave of Enlightenment criticism of religion? What
about Marx, Freud, Weber, and the best of the twentieth century
social scientists? On this point Smart had little to say except to
reassert in heteronomous fashion the adequacy of church tradition.
Consequently his interpretation of the seeming truce between
neo-orthodox theology and the social sciences was not persuasive.
To sum it up: James Smart failed to comprehend the depth of the
theological crisis which B. A. Gerrish recently defined so suc-
cinctly: ". . . it is not so much that the tradition itself has been
corrupted by the infidelity of the church as that the church's tradition in the modern world has become insecure."[21]

My second criticism of Smart also reflects the insights of scholars whose work was not available when he wrote **The Teaching Ministry of the Church.** For the most part he concentrated largely on one mode of ministry, the ministry to God's Word. Yet as Bernard Cooke has implied in such a provocative manner, there are educational dimensions to all of the various forms of ministry, particularly in "Ministry as Formation of Community," or "Ministering to God's Judgment."[22] Smart's preoccupation with the ministry to God's Word did not allow him to mount an effective critique of the managerial image of ministry that so dominated the thinking of the earlier promoters of the DRE. Instead, he substituted the notion of the teacher (often didactically oriented) in place of the educator as manager without criticizing the latter concept. In contrast, H. Richard Niebuhr, who was writing **The Purpose of the Church and Its Ministry** at the same time, moved in a different direction. By exploring the phrase, "pastoral director," Niebuhr was both acknowledging the reality of the changing form of ministry in the latter part of the nineteenth and early twentieth centuries and also stressing the imperative need for **transforming** the modern world's understanding of administration.[23]

But while it is dated, Smart's book remains as a reminder of a neglected task that needs to be taken up in the coming decade. Both Catholics and Protestants can now understand the respective claims of tradition and modernity by learning from each other. The old topic of "Ministry and Education" has new possibilities. If we follow this trail to its end, we will encounter, sooner or later, the challenge implied in Werner Jaeger's quiet conclusion: "Therefore, education in any human community . . . is the direct expression of its active awareness of a **standard.**" What is our standard, our ministry? And can we express that ministry in a way that is faithful, in Gerrish's words, to the "dual norm of fidelity to tradition and intelligibility in the modern world?"[24] Those will be important questions to ask in the 1980s.

NOTES

1. James D. Smart, **The Teaching Ministry of the Church: An Examination of the Basic Principles of Christian Education** (Philadelphia: The Westminster Press, 1954).

2. Werner Jaeger, **Paideia: The Ideals of Greek Culture** (Washington Square, NY: New York University Press, 1945), vol. 1, p. xiv.

3. B. A. Gerrish, **Tradition and the Modern World: Reformed Theology in the Nineteenth Century** (Chicago: The University of Chicago Press, 1978), p. 7.

4. Bernard Cooke, **Ministry to Word and Sacraments: History and Theology** (Philadelphia: Fortress Press, 1976).

5. W. H. Boocock, "Director of Religious Education," **The Encyclopedia of Sunday Schools and Religious Education** (New York: Thomas Nelson & Sons, 1915), vol. 1, p. 348.

6. Ibid.

7. Ibid., p. 350.

8. William Rainey Harper, **The Trend in Higher Education** (Chicago: The University of Chicago Press, 1905), p. 198.

9. Ibid., p. 203.

10. Ibid., p. 229.

11. Ibid., p. 227.

12. Ibid., p. 228.

13. Laurence R. Veysey, **The Emergence of the American University** (Chicago: The University of Chicago Press, 1965), pp. 370-372. Veysey noted the similarity between his fascination with the structure of the Hebrew language and the structure of institutions.

14. Washington Gladden, **The Christian Pastor and the Working Church** (New York: Charles Scribner's & Sons, 1898), pp. 8-9.

15. Robert H. Wiebe, **The Search for Order: 1877-1920** (New York: Hill and Wang, 1967), p. 295.

16. Ibid., p. 111f.

17. George Albert Coe, **A Social Theory of Religious Education** (New York: Charles Scribner's Sons, 1917), p. 279.

18. Ibid., p. 280.

19. C. Ellis Nelson, **Where Faith Begins** (Richmond: John Knox Press, 1967).

20. Smart, p. 113.

21. Gerrish, p. 7.

22. See Cooke, p. 33f. and p. 405f.

23. H. Richard Niebuhr, **The Purpose of the Church and Its Ministry: Reflections on the Aims of Theological Education** (New York: Harper & Row, 1956).

24. Gerrish, p. 7.

QUESTIONS FOR DISCUSSION

1) What, in your own view, qualifies one to minister? What would be your definition of a "learned ministry"?

2) Lynn recounts some of the factors at work in Protestant denominations which led to the DRE position. Which of these factors do you see as also being operative in Catholicism in recent years? Which factors might be unique to a Catholic setting?

3) The evolution of the Protestant minister from preacher to manager meant that ministers came to be viewed as "pastoral directors" and as organizers of the community. Such a perspective, Lynn implies, is inadequate in dealing with both tradition and modernity. Both Schneiders and Butler speak of the ministry of the ordained as one of "ordering." Is "ordering" the Catholic equivalent of "pastoral director"?

4) Lynn argues that DREs have, as a group, not yet achieved the "cohesion of a serious professional association" or "parity with other ministers" because of their "inability to grasp a sufficiently comprehensive and compelling interpretation of ministry." What sort of preparation and continuing education might help DREs today to avoid this "failure of vision"?

5) Roman Catholic DREs are recent arrivals in comparison with their Protestant colleagues. What might they learn from them?

6) In Lynn's critique of biblical theologian James Smart, he comments that Smart's preoccupation with the ministry to God's Word led him to ignore other forms of ministry. How should the ministry of Word and sacraments be viewed in relationship to each other? What differences in this relationship, if any, might be characteristic of Protestant and Catholic perspectives?

7) In what way do you see the minister functioning in the tension between tradition and modernity? The educator?

Ministry and Education:
Some Critical Reflections

by Richard P. McBrien

AUTOBIOGRAPHICAL STATEMENT

It is with a certain measure of diffidence that I approach the task of providing some autobiographical introduction. I have been through this exercise twice already in recent years and I am convinced that there is very little more to be said. One or two interested readers may want to track down my contribution to **Journeys: The Impact of Personal Experience on Religious Thought,** edited by Gregory Baum (New York: Paulist Press, 1975), pp. 255-71, or my later essay "On Being a Catholic" in **Why Catholic?,** edited by John J. Delaney (New York: Doubleday, 1979), pp. 115-36.

Briefly, I was fascinated with politics before I ever became involved with theology, and I am reasonably sure that I would never have gone into theology had I not been attracted from my earliest years to the Catholic priesthood. My initial theological interests were, not surprisingly, related to issues of social justice and the reform of political and economic institutions. Gradually that blending of politics and theology found a more focused home in ecclesiology. Most of my theological writing, teaching, and lecturing, therefore, have been addressed to questions related to the mystery of the Church: mission, authority, ministries, ecumenism, and so forth.

I became even more attentive to the relationship of religious education to theology as my association with Boston College's Institute of Religious Education and Pastoral Ministry developed from pioneer faculty member to director. And in the last two years, with the preparation of my two-volume work, **Catholicism** (Minneapolis: Winston Press, 1980), I also deliberately expanded my range of theological reflection to embrace the whole sweep of the Catholic tradition. In that ambitious enterprise I assumed the considerable risk of attempting a comprehensive and integrated exposition. It is within the larger context of that effort that readers of this volume might make even better sense of what I am driving at in this essay than the essay itself may reveal.

Richard P. McBrien

This symposium raised some of the right questions and to that extent was a success. To be sure, such an assertion has the ring of a cliché. The claim that it is more important to raise the right questions than to discover the right answers often reflects an assumption that truth is so relative (not just relational) and so elusive that one person's version of it is as good or as bad as any other's. Such a mentality encourages anti-intellectualism by serving as a justification for undisciplined thought or even laziness. Although I do not accept this assumption about the relativity and elusiveness of truth, it is evident that the raising of the right questions **is** a necessary precondition for discovering the right answers. Moreover one has also to acknowledge that our answers are already implied in the kinds of questions we ask and in the way we pose them.

I. THE QUESTIONS

I note four major clusters of questions which emerged during the course of the symposium. The first had to do with identity—the identity of the religious educator and the identity of the minister. The second had to do with community and the necessity of the community's call to ministry. The third had to do with culture and with the way in which it shapes our understanding and exercise of ministry. And the fourth had to do with spirituality, that is, with the way in which faith, hope, and love shape our understanding and exercise of ministry.

1. **The identity questions.** There was a consensus within the symposium that religious education (however defined) is a ministry (however defined). How is the practice of religious education

qualified by its ministerial character? Is religious education always and only a ministry? Is there anything about religious education which is proper to it and which is not at the same time ministerial in character? Do new models of education have any impact on the way we exercise the various other pastoral ministries? In other words, what does ministry have to learn from education?

2. **The community questions.** What function does the call of the community (through ordination or some other means) have in the authentication or certification of particular ministries? Is the vocation to ministry, which is in principle universal, to be exercised simply at the discretion of the individual herself or himself, or does the community within which and for which the ministry would be exercised have the responsibility and therefore the right to determine who should in fact exercise ministry on its behalf? What is to be said about the sacramentality of certain ministries?

3. **The culture questions.** To what extent does culture shape our understanding and exercise of ministry, including religious education? To what extent are theology and doctrine at issue? To what extent, for example, is the present exclusion of, and attitude toward, women in ordained ministry a reflection of cultural consciousness? To what extent is it also a reflection of theological and doctrinal presuppositions? To what extent, in the final accounting, are the theological and the doctrinal influenced by the cultural, and vice versa?

4. **The spirituality questions.** Is there some radical incompatibility between ministry and professionalism? What does the minister's (or indeed any Christian's) call to poverty imply? What does identification with the poor mean? What do faith, hope, and love—or for that matter any of the cardinal virtues of prudence, justice, temperance, and fortitude—have to do with the exercise of ministry? What are the criteria for an integral Christian spirituality for the Church's ministers and how are the criteria to be applied in the recruitment, selection, and ongoing evaluation of these ministers?

At the risk of imposing an artificial framework on the four panelists' papers, I shall provide some brief critical comment on each of their contributions in light of these four clusters of questions. I shall also offer some similarly abbreviated remarks about the discussion process in which the registered participants engaged.

II. THE PANELISTS

1. Sandra Schneiders

The focus of Sandra Schneiders' paper was on the ministry of the Word. This ministry is not simply **one** of the Church's many ministries. The New Testament, she insisted, leaves little doubt that it is the Church's **primary** ministry. Indeed, Jesus himself was recognized as a prophet and a teacher, and understood his mission in terms of "bearing witness to the truth" (John 18:37), preaching (Mark 1:38), and evangelizing the poor (Matt. 11:5).

This primacy of the Word, however, has nothing to do with intellectualism or with gnostic notions of salvation. Rather, it arises from the fact that faith must be evoked, nurtured, sustained, and challenged by the witness of the disciples who themselves are persons of faith pointing to the presence and action of God in human experience.

In Catholic theology, catechesis, and preaching, the notion of faith became progressively less a matter of commitment and more a matter of assent to truths. Although Protestants always emphasized the former, they found no real alternative to the school model of the ministry of the Word because commitment is not readily translated into tangible categories. Accordingly, Protestants pursued a somewhat ambivalent course in religious education, while Catholics persisted in the path of indoctrination, or something akin to it.

In light of recent changes within Catholic theology, how can the relationship of faith and ministry be understood? Sandra Schneiders has suggested that faith is the integral response to God's saving action on our behalf and that it is most alive and effective in small grassroots communities. Faith operates there as a kind of hermeneutic, allowing people to interpret their everyday experience and then to put that interpretation to use for personal and social transformation. Faith, therefore, is a way of looking at the human reality in the light of the Gospel.

Education is a dimension of the ministry of the Word and, as such, its function is to serve faith. But education is not confined to the classroom or the pulpit. It also takes place in the street, the factory, on the farm, in the coffee shop, and so forth. Because the Word of God became flesh, the ministry of the Word, including education, must seek new incarnations of itself in every age, incarnations that correspond to the faith experience of each new age.

In less formal remarks during the symposium itself, Sandra Schneiders fixed much of her attention on the ordination question, and she has returned to it in her "Afterword." The call to ministry is universal, she reminded us, and is communicated in Baptism. We must not exaggerate ordination. Ordained ministry is not the only ministry, nor is it the source of authority for all other ministries. Most ministries, in fact, do not even require ordination. Credentialing is important, of course, but it should always be done in a participative way rather than in an hierarchical manner. The latter approach assumes that inequality in the Church is ordained by God and that the community is structured in accordance with some divine institutional plan. The participative approach, on the contrary, assumes a fundamental equality within the Church and insists that differences are based on factors other than juridical authority. Insofar as there are different ministries, they represent different spheres of ministry (the one meeting this need here, another meeting that need over there) rather than different levels of ministry (the one greater than the other).

Although Sandra Schneiders has made clear her understanding and definition of Christian education (note 1), one finds no similarly precise definition of ministry. She has paid well-deserved tribute to Bernard Cooke's massive **Ministry to Word and Sacraments** (note 11), but remarkably Cooke himself nowhere discloses his own working definition of ministry. Vagueness, perhaps even ambiguity, are allowed to stand. The identity questions, therefore, are only partially addressed and answered.

Secondly, so straightforward had been Sandra Schneiders' criticism of the hierarchical model that some of the symposium registrants began moving toward the conclusion that ordination is of no real consequence in the celebration of the Eucharist. When pressed for clarification, she readily agreed that the mere desire to preside at the Eucharist or the encouragement of one's friends and associates are never sufficient in themselves to justify the exercise of such a ministry. On the one hand, ordination was not always required for such a ministry in the New Testament. On the other hand, some form of community call was implied in its exercise.

But what constitutes "community" or Church in this context? Why is the initiation into some ministries also a sacramental act? How is the sacramentality of these ministries consistent with the assertion that ministries differ only in terms of spheres and never in terms of levels of importance? If the ministry of the Word is primary, by what process is the meaning of that Word determined? Are there levels, not just spheres, of interpretation so that some sources of interpretation are more authoritative for the whole Church than others? If so, what are these levels, and what criteria do we have to determine their relative authority?

Sandra Schneiders has begun answering some of these questions in her helpfully instructive "Afterword," where she distinguishes between ordained ministry as "a particular function in the Church, namely that of leadership with its special service to the apostolicity, unity, and mission of the community," and presiding over the Eucharist which may or may not require ordination in every instance. She argues against ordaining everyone who is to preside unless the presider is also to be commissioned with pastoral leadership responsibilities. Those who would act as "special presidents" (e.g., religious superiors, heads of households, retreatants) would do so on an ad hoc basis only, for reasons which she has provided in the "Afterword" itself. One can support the main lines of her arguments and proposals and at the same time regret that the limitations of space and perhaps an occasional excess of style might render her "Afterword" less persuasive to initially unsympathetic readers.

Thirdly, although there is much justifiable criticism of the indoctrination mentality of the Counter-Reformation and pre-Vatican II Catholic Church, there is no explicit recognition that the meaning and forms of the alternative "commitment" are themselves culturally conditioned. Sandra Schneiders has argued that faith is most alive and effective in small grassroots communities, but precisely what kind of faith is it? What criteria are we to employ in determining its vitality and its effectiveness? If faith is an interpretation of reality "in the light of the Gospel," through which process(es) is the Gospel assimilated, understood, interpreted, and applied? If the indoctrination school was culturally conditioned in its approach, why is not the commitment school also conditioned? How does this conditioning affect the final product? On what basis can these conditioning processes be critiqued?

Fourthly, in resisting Virgil Elizondo's suggestion that ministry and professionalism may be incompatible, Sandra Schneiders stimulated some reexamination of conventional assumptions concerning spirituality. Is ministry to be open only to celibates or to those without substantial economic responsibilities? However admirable a figure she may be, Mother Teresa cannot serve as a model for every minister of the Church. And yet because of the incarnational principle, God's self-communication must be witnessed in order to be perceived. As the word of God finds a home in the one to whom witness is given, this disciple in turn becomes a witness by word and life to others. But what criteria can we use in evaluating the quality of such witnessing? Sandra Schneiders might fruitfully address this question elsewhere. She is clearly competent to do so.

2. Virgil Elizondo

It was Virgil Elizondo's thesis that the intersection of ministry and education in the Church is determined by the interplay among anthropology, ecclesiology, and christology. As Catholic notions of these three theological areas have developed from pre-Vatican II days, through the council itself, and finally up to the present, our understanding of the relationship between education and ministry has progressively changed.

In the pre-Vatican II period inequality was accepted as an ordinary way of life. Classism and racism prevailed. The same inequality also characterized the life of the Church, which understood itself as a perfect society, hierarchically structured. Only the clergy had the power to minister and to educate (what Elizondo apparently identified with the teaching of "religion"). The underlying christological emphasis of this pre-Vatican II mentality was on the divinity of Christ: a Christ of power, the Christ who would judge us all, the Christ who legitimates both the structures of the Church and of society.

About the time of Vatican II many peoples of the world began rejecting their unequal status. They looked upon the concept of development as a way of making all the "backward" nations "like us," that is, like the white, Western population of the world. The Church, too, began emphasizing service as development.

New professional classes emerged: religious educators, campus ministers, theologians, and so forth. Certification provided a kind of ordination into a new priestly clique. Ministry was doing things for people in a professional way and at professional wages. Only those who became professionalized could exercise ministry in the Church. Correspondingly, there was a new emphasis on Jesus Christ as Son of Man, as one of us and one with us. But he became for many simply a "nice guy" who would never move us to challenge the world's enslaving structures.

With the emergence of Latin American liberation theology at Medellin in 1968, and with the election of Pope John Paul II in 1978 and his historic visit to Mexico the following January, oppressed people began affirming themselves for what they are, refusing to be classified as inferior and in need of development. Traditional education was increasingly perceived as enslaving rather than liberating. Minorities recognized the importance of establishing their own institutions and of preserving their own ethnic values and practices. While the churches of the North Atlantic were struggling to renew their liturgical celebrations, their religious education programs, and their many ministries of service to the People of God, the churches of the Third World were struggling to engage fully in the process of liberation.

And now the tables are turned, Virgil Elizondo declared. It is the less fortunate who will initiate the liberation and salvation of the more fortunate ones of the world. It is to the Church of the poor and for the poor that the future belongs. Although the Church still needs ordained ministers and well-qualified professionals, they need to be in solidarity with the poor of the world, entering into their existence, listening to them with great love, and assuming their misery and their struggles. The final verification of the authenticity and legitimacy of the Christian minister, he insisted, is neither ordination nor a degree, but the holiness and fidelity of lifestyle. In this new and present context, it is the kenotic Christ, the Christ who emptied himself (Phil. 2:5-11), to whom the Church must look. The issue is not **who** Jesus is, but **how** did he live? Jesus lived in solidarity with the poor and the oppressed and died as a political subversive. It is only in the full appreciation of the **kenosis,** Virgil Elizondo concluded, that we will avoid the dichotomies of an overemphasis either on the divinity or on the humanity of Christ.

With regard to the identity questions, Virgil Elizondo relied surprisingly on a dictionary for his definitions of both ministry and education. And yet in subsequent discussion he would argue that one cannot make a definition of anything because we do not even know what a definition means. One is led reluctantly to the suspicion that some anti-intellectual spirit runs through his paper. Professionals are referred to as the "new high priests," "a new hierarchy," invested at times even with a measure of infallibility. Such professionals package and control a body of knowledge for their own well-being and survival and maintain an absolute monopoly on the certification process for other professionals. Indeed, these professionals are themselves among the principal exploiters of the poor by legitimating oppressive academic institutions and other systems of exploitation. Over against such élitist prejudices, Virgil Elizondo argued, we must defend the right of everyone to speak and to be taken seriously. No one is any more authoritative, reliable, or credible than anyone else.

Consistently with this view, Virgil Elizondo stressed that ministry is universal. Everyone has something to offer. Standards and criteria are apparently not to be imposed, whether they be based on ordination or on academic certification. But one is compelled to ask him whether there are any ministries at all which place the very identity of the Church on the line? If so, what role should the community have in authenticating the call to such ministries as these? What criteria should the Church employ in the recruitment, selection, and ongoing evaluation of those who feel themselves called? In other words, who decides, and on what basis, who enters ordained ministry? And beyond the sacramental ministries, should there be a religious education program in a parish, for example? If so, should it be a coordinated program? If so, who determines the curriculum? Who selects and supervises the facilitators of learning? How is their pastoral and educational effectiveness measured?

Secondly, with regard to the question of the Church's role in the call to ministry, the one Protestant panelist, Robert Lynn, observed that Virgil Elizondo seemed to him more Baptist than Catholic. Specifically, Elizondo had argued that ministry is authenticated not by office or by competence but by holiness and by fidelity of lifestyle. It is a priesthood of all believers in the classic Reformation sense, and a defense and celebration of local sovereignty over against the Church universal that would, according to Lynn, do credit to the most devoted Baptist. In subsequent discussion, Elizondo reminded the symposium that community can be just as oppressive as hierarchy, and that the hierarchical model (referring here to Sandra Schneiders' distinction between the hierarchical and the participative) can also be liberating. It is the bishop who sends the priest. The priest's authority is, therefore, secure over against the community and over against the government. One might wonder if this belated appeal to the hierarchical principle reflects some underlying ecclesiological ambivalence.

Thirdly, Virgil Elizondo was strongest in his insistence on the cultural dimension of Christian faith and practice. He called attention to the challenge of integrating the major cultural moments in the life of a people with their experience, understanding, and celebration of Christian faith, for instance, devotion to Our Lady of Guadalupe, Thanksgiving, the Christmas crib. How do we transmit the faith today in light of the people's needs, he asked? We need to hear more from Virgil Elizondo precisely on this point. We should also want to hear him reflect more than he apparently has on the culturally conditioned, and therefore inevitably limited, character of all theology, including liberation theology, and of all critiques of human experience, including even the critique of society of the sort he shared with us.

Fourthly, although Virgil Elizondo stressed more than any other panelist the need for developing an appropriate spirituality for various ministries in the Church, he may have unwittingly muddied the waters with his suggestion that some radical incompatibility exists between ministry and professionalism—a suggestion accompanied by the acknowledgment of the Church's right to have competent ministers. Furthermore, his moving advocacy of the cause of the poor did not explicitly recognize the relativity of the reality of poverty or the universality of sin. It is as if the poor are not to be evangelized except as a process of consciousness-raising so that they will see themselves as victims of institutionalized oppression. God presumably speaks a word of judgment **through** the poor, but never **to** the poor. Indeed, for Virgil Elizondo wealth itself is sinful. But again he seems not to have acknowledged the relativity of wealth nor to define it more precisely. Is Pope John Paul II, whom he warmly approved, truly poor? Is the pope economically deprived or dependent? Is his poverty reflected in his residence, in the fact that many minister to him daily, in his freedom to travel, in his eating habits, in his wardrobe?

The development of an appropriate spirituality is an abiding challenge for each of the Church's ministers, but it is a spirituality which has to do with more than the divisions of rich and poor, oppressor and oppressed, however important these divisions might be to the process of evangelization. What are the criteria for an integral Christian spirituality for the Church's ministers, and how are they to be applied in their recruitment, selection, and ongoing evaluation? These are the kinds of fundamental questions theologians, religious educators, and other pastoral ministers must address at once, and Virgil Elizondo can be a valuable partner in our common search for answers.

3. Sara Butler

It would appear that Sara Butler's overall approach is similar to Virgil Elizondo's. She, too, wants to get "beyond professionalism" and broaden the reality of ministry to include everyone who renders loving and caring service, without at the same time institutionalizing ministry to the point of bringing all forms of it under ecclesiastical supervision and control.

She suggested in her paper that education has suffered for not being perceived enough as a ministry, and that ministry has suffered for being identified too much with ordained priesthood. Contemporary reflection on the New Testament and the early history of the Church alike disclose this broader understanding of ministry, while the needs of people themselves are forcing us to develop a broader understanding of education.

Ministry, she argued, is the "umbrella term under which true Christian education falls." Education is "ministry under the specific formality of proclamation, reflection, clarification, and integration of understanding." The two intersect in the parish catechumenate. The process of Christian initiation involves education insofar as the tradition is passed on from the sponsors to the catechumens. But it is also ministry insofar as the sponsors are present and available to the catechumens as supportive, believing persons, engaged in a common quest for meaning.

In subsequent discussion among the panelists and in dialogue with the symposium registrants, Sara Butler insisted that her understanding of ministry is not so wide that it includes every form of human service. Ministry is a public function, involving some stable role, demanding some measure of competence, and is authenticated by the call of some ecclesial community to which the minister remains accountable. On the other hand, ministry always requires personal assimilation. It is holiness in action. It is never a neutral or purely professional activity.

Sara Butler was clearly attentive to the complexity of defining ministry and of differentiating it from religious education. She acknowledged that the word ministry has both a universal and a particular meaning, that it applies to ordained and non-ordained forms of service alike, and that every form of it is educational in some sense in that it is directed always toward human growth and development. On the other hand, her discussion of ministry tended to focus more on the interpersonal than on the social, the political, or the institutional. A service rendered to another becomes a ministry, she wrote, when it is "consciously set in relation to one's personal knowledge of God, life of faith, struggle with prayer." The "basic model for this style is really counseling, or what Nouwen classified as 'individual pastoral care.' " She speaks of the new interest in pastoral ministry graduate programs in terms of this same model of "individual pastoral care" and its "commitment to interpersonal relationships."

A similar problem emerges in her treatment of education. Although she noted that education is both socializing and liberating, she assigned a relatively narrow meaning to the term "liberation." "Education as liberation," she declared, "facilitates the dialogue with reality in which a person can come to full potential as creator of her own destiny." The social, political, and institutional dimensions of understanding, interpretation, growth, and development are not explicitly accounted for. The emphasis again is on the personal and the interpersonal.

Religious educators will also resist the findings of her concluding paragraph on the relationship between ministry and education and ask if she has forgotten her earlier insistence that
education is itself a form of ministry. How, then, can education be
set over against ministry as if it were not itself a form of ministry?
And if education **is** a ministry, why suggest that it is any less
concerned about mutuality, community, or spirituality than any
other form of pastoral ministry?

Sara Butler was commendably forthright in her insistence that
ministry requires a call from some ecclesial community. Her stress
on the personal notwithstanding, ministry is, for her, never so
much a personal enterprise that it can begin and end with the
individual or be exercised on the individual's own terms and according to the individual's own desires and designs. Indeed, Sara
Butler engaged in a relatively spirited discussion with Sandra
Schneiders and others precisely on the necessity of ordination for
the exercise of the ministry of presiding at the Eucharist. She
touched more than any of the other panelists on the sacramentality
of certain ministries, and on the qualitative difference such sacramentality creates in those ministries. But time and circumstance
did not permit a very substantial elaboration upon these themes.

The third of the cluster questions had to do with the cultural
dimension of ministry and of education. Sara Butler acknowledged
that a community hands on not only its wisdom but also its culture
and that this is the essence of education. The suggestive point is
not developed, however, even though there is a passing reference
to the **communidades de base** which are renewing the Church from
below. Indeed, the culturally conditioned character of all ministry
and education is not explicitly mentioned at all.

It was on the spirituality question that Sara Butler may have
made her strongest contribution. The apparent inconsistency of the
final paragraph notwithstanding, her paper firmly situated education under the umbrella of ministry, with all that this implies.
Ministry brings a particular intentionality to education. It is a
matter of "being attentive to another in faith." Because the educator
is also and always a minister, the educator "lends his or her own
experience of God in faith to the other, supporting the other in a
very personal way." Ministry is, as she suggested later, holiness in
action. But again the emphasis is on the personal and the interpersonal, and less on the social, the political, and the institutional. A

spirituality that is integrally Christian because it is also integrally human has to have that wider dimension as well.

4. Robert Lynn

Robert Lynn's paper is the most difficult of the four to summarize. It is a sophisticated historical essay, such as one might reasonably expect from a sophisticated historian of religious education. He reviewed the story of the rise and fall of the Director of Religious Education in American Protestantism ("It does not have a happy ending," he informed his audience) and suggests that much of Protestantism's problem was linked with its failure to define more precisely what it meant by ministry and how any ministry, including that of the religious educator, can do justice at one and the same time to the tradition and to modernity. In general, Protestant religious education has sinned by excess more in favor of modernity than of the tradition. He warned that Roman Catholics would be well advised to attend critically to the Protestant experience and not to make the Protestant mistake of allowing itself to become a "hostage to the pretensions of modernity."

How can this be done? If education is, according to Werner Jaeger, "the direct expression of [a community's] active awareness of a **standard**," we must ask what is **our** standard for ministry? Furthermore, "can we express that ministry in a way that is faithful . . . to the 'dual norm of fidelity to tradition and intelligibility in the modern world'?"

Robert Lynn, perhaps more than any of the other panelists, ranged widely beyond his paper in the symposium discussions. He agreed with the others that we have to go beyond professionalism, but by what theological criteria do we do that? Can we finally escape modernity, he asked? Can we be excellent and equal at the same time? When the tradition is insecure, as it is today, we tend to embrace premature heteronomous certitudes. If ministry is everything, he argued, it is nothing. If the faith that must inform ministry is only personal and interpersonal in character, as traditional Protestantism always described it, what of the content of faith and the requirements of conceptual clarity? How are we to avoid the other Protestant tendency toward historical discontinuity? If we are not to become prisoners of the present moment, the tradition must be allowed to interpret and transform present experience. Finally, what of the institutional and sacramental dimensions of the community of faith? Are we not, he asked, in danger of divorcing them from our more personalist and interpersonalist understandings of Church?

Robert Lynn raised such questions from outside the Roman Catholic tradition, almost as if to say again and again, "Yes, but . . ." Because his contribution was so different from the other three panelists, it is perhaps inappropriate to apply the same test to his presentations as were applied above. He did not offer his own specific answers to the identity questions, but he expressed dissatisfaction with the recent tendency toward a kind of ministrification of the whole Church. He did not specify the role of the community in the call to ministry, but he expressed concern about the way in which the institutional and the communitarian were being divorced in some of the discussions. He did not provide an outline for a ministerial spirituality, but he raised questions about the theological criteria according to which such a spirituality would be developed. It was in the area of culture that Robert Lynn seemed to focus most sharply because it was there, in his discussion of the impact of modernity upon tradition, that he began and ended his formal paper, and it was this concern that he used as a point of reference for his extended remarks in the symposium itself. He did not, in the end, identify the standard by which present Christian experience is to be judged; he urged only that we recognize the need for a standard which is independent of the shifting tides of contemporary thought.

III. THE PROCESS

A discussion format, such as the symposium adopted, is not infallibly preferable to one based primarily on input from competent resource persons. The discussion approach can sometimes lead participants to believe that one person's view of a theological or pastoral issue, such as ministry, is as good as another's. But this is manifestly not always the case. Some bring greater knowledge and understanding to a particular issue than others.

What each participant **does** uniquely bring, of course, is his or her own experience as well as the assorted impressions and reflections which flow from that experience: What do I do? What do I think I should be doing? What problems do I face in my work? What might improve my situation? But there is more to a discussion than the sharing of one's own experience. To think and act as if there are no standards beyond one's own personal experience and one's reflection on that experience is to be imprisoned by that experience.

Thus, we need not, and ought not, take seriously a definition or understanding of ministry offered by someone who is obviously innocent of the meaning and significance of such historical items as these: the break from Judaism at the Council of Jerusalem in the year 50 (the circumcision question) and the missionary move from Jerusalem itself to the Gentile world, especially Corinth; the development of the monarchical episcopate in the second century (Ignatius of Antioch); the Apostolic Tradition of Hippolytus of Rome (third century) with its ordination rites for bishops (drawn from the New Testament notion of pastoral ministry), for presbyters (drawn from Old Testament notions), and for deacons; the Edict of Constantine in 312 and the emergence of a separate and privileged clerical class; the Germanization of Christianity in the early Middle Ages and the impact of feudalism on ordained ministry; the Council of Trent and the Reformation; and the content of the various ecumenical dialogues since Vatican II.

It is precisely this lack of an historical sense that prevents both the right and the left in the Church from perceiving correctly such thorny issues as the necessity of ordination for priestly ministry. The right seems not to realize that there is no hard evidence in the New Testament for the thesis that ordination is always required for presiding at the Eucharist, that indeed non-ordained Christians have heard confessions in the past and still are ministers of the sacrament of Matrimony. Ordination is for the sake of order, not for the sake of conferring some magical power. The left, on the other hand, seems not to have noticed that there is more ministerial structure in the New Testament and the early Church than the lower-church traditions have acknowledged. As Anglican Bishop John A. T. Robinson once insisted: "It is impossible to be a biblical theologian without being a high Churchman." Furthermore, ordination is a sacramental act. It has more than organizational significance. It symbolizes and celebrates the reality of Church to an extent that non-sacramental ministries do not. As Sandra Schneiders reminds us in her "Afterword," ordination initiates the Christian into a particular ministerial relationship with the Church. The ordained ministry is a special service to the unity, apostolicity, and catholicity of the Church. The life and mission of the Church are engaged in the ordained minister's service in ways that are not simply duplicated in the other ministries. This is not to say, of course, that such ordained ministries should be open only to celibate males or that they should carry with them forms of jurisdictional authority that place every other ministry under their direct control.

Here again we are raising more questions than we can answer. The hope is that they are the right kind of questions and that we are posing them in the right way.

But that is what this symposium was all about in the first place.

Index

INDEX OF SUBJECTS

as hermeneutic, 24-25
as intellectual assent, 21, 23, 39n.14
as personal commitment to Jesus,
    23-24
primacy of ministry of Word and, 20
as service, 83
as witness, 19-20

"Grassroots" communities. **See** Basic
    communities

Liberation model, 58
Liberation theology, 25, 122

Magisterium, 50
    co-ministry of magisteria, 28, 40n.27
Marxism, 49
Medellin, 47, 120
Metanoia. **See** Conversion
Minister
    as local theologian, 105
    as pastoral director, 103-105, 109
Ministry. **See also** Ordination
    of acolyte, 86
    as apostleship and evangelization, 21
    of catechist, 86
    catechumenate and, 79-80, 123-124
    Catholic schools and, 22, 24
    charisms and, 50, 66, 92n.13
    contemplation and, 82
    defined, 10-11, 48, 79, 81, 123-124
    diversity of ministries and, 17-18, 37,
        84
    of DRE, 102
    educational dimensions and, 109
    as evangelization, 21
    of Jesus, 17, 68-69, 83
    of liberation, 61, 83
    lifestyle of poverty and, 64-65
    managerial image and, 102-107, 109
    of music, 86
    not equivalent with priesthood, 81
    of the ordained, 27, 34-37, 84-85, 87,
        129
    of reader, 86
    to serve faith, 25
    service and, 54-55, 83
    as service of interpretation, 24-25
    solidarity with the poor and, 65-66
    of the theologian, 28
    as "umbrella term" for Christian
        education, 11, 18, 89-90, 123
    women and, 28, 86, 115, 129
    of the Word, 17-25, 116

Ordination
    economic dimension of, 30-31

ministry and, 27, 34-37, 84-85, 87,
    117, 129
political dimension of, 28-30
professional dimension of, 26-28,
    49-50, 55, 67
sacramental dimension of, 32-37, 118,
    125

Paideia, 98-100, 109, 126
Pastoral care, 82, 90, 124
Pastoral director. **See** Minister
Poverty
    commitment of Church to poor, 59-62
    evangelical, 63, 72n.15
    lifestyle and, 64-65
    as structural, 59-60
Priesthood. **See** Ordination
Professionalism
    in developmental model, 52-53
    era of professional church workers,
        53-54
    financial remuneration and, 26, 30-31,
        54-55, 64-65
    ministerial credentialing and, 26-28,
        30-31, 49, 87, 115, 121
    need to transcend, 63, 82, 123, 126
Puebla, 48, 60, 72n.12, 73n.20

Racism, 49-50, 51, 119
Religious education
    defined, 13n.7
    Roman Catholic documents on
        General Catechetical Directory,
            13n.7
        Sharing the Light of Faith, 13n.7
        To Teach as Jesus Did, 92n.21

Religious instruction, defined, 13n.7

Salvation
    as carried to world by the poor, 62
    defined, 18-19
Socialization, 88-89
Spiritual direction, 82
Spirituality, 10, 50, 65, 115, 119, 122-123,
    125

Third World, 56-59, 71n.9, 120

Women in ministry. **See** Ministry